A PENGUIN SPECIAL

S201

THE GENERAL SAYS NO

Britain's Exclusion from Europe

NORA BELOFF

The General Says No

BRITAIN'S EXCLUSION FROM EUROPE

NORA BELOFF

PENGUIN BOOKS

Penguin Books Ltd, Harmondsworth, Middlesex
U.S.A.: Penguin Books Inc., 3300 Clipper Mill Road, Baltimore 11, Md
AUSTRALIA: Penguin Books Pty Ltd, 762 Whitehorse Road,
Mitcham, Victoria

—

First published 1963

—

Copyright © Nora Beloff, 1963

—

Made and printed in Great Britain
by Cox and Wyman Ltd
London, Reading, and Fakenham
Set in Monotype Times

CONTENTS

FOREWORD

WHAT hit us? For almost two years the British people have been re-examining their national identity. Are we still a great power? Is there any reality left in the old notions of national sovereignty, patriotism, Commonwealth leadership, and military independence? If not, should the British surrender a large slab of public business to a Community in which they would be minority partners only? Are there other more appropriate international groupings, or should Britain accept irrevocable links with Western Europe, that small exposed peninsula, with its tremendous human resources and peculiar capacity for self-destruction, at the tip of the Eurasian landmass?

To answer these questions has proved agonizingly difficult. When the Conservative Party came round to saying 'yes' to the European Community, Labour leaders charged them with turning their backs on a thousand years of history: the Conservatives retaliated by claiming that the future was on their side – at which the reviving Liberal Party protested that they had been for joining Europe all the time. And then, while the country was still locked in argument and passions were red hot, General de Gaulle said 'No', and Britain's own views on her national destiny suddenly appeared absurdly irrelevant.

How could we have presented him with such an exposed posterior? Was the whole debate a gigantic hoax, with the French never intending to let us in? Why did the General pronounce the verdict as unexpectedly and brutally as he did?

As I reported the story of the breakdown in the columns of the *Observer* I became aware there were still many unsolved mysteries. The chapters in this book are the results of an attempt to discover the answers.

First, what kind of man was de Gaulle, what was he after, and why was he hostile to Britain? And then, on the British side, after saying so long and so loud that Britain could never join the European Economic Community, why did the Prime Minister perform such a startling somersault? And once the Government did want to go in, why did the Conference get bogged down for so long over bacon subsidies and tinned salmon? Were the negotiations really on the brink of success when they were interrupted, as Macmillan alleged, or was de Gaulle right in saying there were still insurmountable obstacles?

Nor were the riddles only Anglo–French: why, when the Germans had so persistently agitated for Britain's entry did they go and sign a Franco–German friendship treaty barely a week after the General had thrown Britain out? Even more mysterious, why did President Kennedy and the Prime Minister meet at Nassau and agree on revolutionary plans for Nato's nuclear future, without first consulting France? Surely they knew de Gaulle held it in his power to demolish not only Macmillan's foreign policy but also Kennedy's 'Grand Design' – the plan for an indissoluble transatlantic partnership between the enlarged European Community and the United States?

The sifting of the evidence involves much more than the behind-the-scene story of the Common Market negotiations. It raises political and defence questions, which counted as much in the sequence of events as the strictly economic transactions round the Brussels conference table. To understand what happened and why, we have to plunge back into the history of how Western Europe was united, and what European unity meant to the many different personalities, including de Gaulle and Jean Monnet, who helped to make the European community what it now is.

The problems examined in this book are still very much with us: the rupture in Brussels has settled nothing, and Britain's re-examination of its new role in the world is still incomplete. But this book is not a tract for or against closer links with Europe; it is a study of the past intended to illuminate Britain's present predicament.

Three ways seem still open to Britain: first, to remain outside any political grouping in Western Europe, while keeping our fingers crossed in the hope that 'the continentals' will not, once again, do anything to upset us. Second, we could make another attempt to get into the kind of European partnership which recommends itself to de Gaulle, in which a group of European states conglomerate, preferably behind him, to form themselves into a single military bloc with its own nuclear power, enabling its leaders, whoever they may be, to qualify once more for big-power status.

Finally there is a third way: to break down the barriers dividing like-minded nations from one another, for the purpose of seeking international solutions to the many problems which confront modern society and seem intractable in the old national setting. Seen in this context, the European Community is a revolutionary experiment and Western Europe only a first stage in the long hard progress towards the management of man's affairs by more rational methods than by the free-for-all struggle between sovereign nation-states whose sole responsibility is to promote the interests of their own citizens – and the devil take care of the rest.

There are in fact two separate questions: one, much debated (though no longer topical), whether Britain should join the European Community; the second, even more important, though rarely examined, what kind of Community will it be? What will its relations be with the other half of the continent which is, after all, also European, and with the developing countries and the outside world?

This story suggests it would have been wiser to tackle the two problems together and, since we cannot draw anchor and sail out of Europe, to see whether we can join in creating the kind of continent which will help promote civilized world order. Or will we let Europe distinguish itself yet again by embroiling the world in a conflict which in this thermo-nuclear age really would be the war to end all wars?

These unfamiliar issues can be understood only by examining the political philosophy and the practical action of the key figures in the story of Britain's tangles with the continent. Without such a study it is impossible to make sense of the European debate which will remain a central issue of British and continental politics in the years immediately ahead. For, as Mr Macmillan told the House of Commons last February, the story of our relations with the European community is not over: 'We are at the end of a chapter, not at the end of a volume.'

Perhaps a little volume is justified all the same, in the hopes that any light on the muddles and misunderstandings of the past two years may help to prevent their renewal at a later stage in the same, continuing story.

This study would have been impossible without the patient and generous help of many cabinet ministers, political leaders, and senior officials from several countries who allowed themselves to be interviewed, and who would no doubt prefer to remain anonymous.

My thanks are due, too, to the *Observer*, in whose service, as a roving correspondent for the past fifteen years, I was able to watch Britain's relations with Europe, not only from London but also from Paris, Washington, Moscow, and many other capitals. In understanding what went wrong, I found it useful to know not only how the outside world looks to us, but also how we look to foreigners.

I am deeply indebted to many of my colleagues on the paper who provided information, practical assistance, and encouragement, and above all to the Deputy Editor, Michael Davie, whose professional help has been invaluable.

The great international fraternity of foreign correspondents has helped me wherever I have been. I owe a special debt to Robert Mauthner, who followed the entire negotiations in Brussels while I watched some of the proceedings from London, Washington, and Paris.

My affectionate thanks are also due to my brother Max, Gladstone Professor of Government and Public Administration at Oxford, without whose advice and incitement this book would not have been written.

NORA BELOFF

London
1 May 1963

CHAPTER ONE

THE EXECUTION

THE death sentence was pronounced on the afternoon of 14 January 1963 in Paris, under the crystal chandeliers of the largest and most ornate reception room in the Élysée Palace, generally known as the Salle des Fêtes. The Jury, Judge, and Counsel for the Prosecution were all incarnate in the imposing, slightly pot-bellied figure of General Charles de Gaulle. The occasion was the General's eighth press conference, and the verdict was without appeal.

The execution was carried out fifteen days later, in the drab offices of the Belgian Foreign Ministry in Brussels. There, the conference for bringing Britain into the Common Market, the most controversial negotiation in British post-war history, which had lasted sixteen months and produced documents by the ton, was formally declared dead.

It was a lugubrious occasion. The seventh floor of the Ministry, graciously lent by the Belgian Foreign Minister, M. Paul-Henri Spaak, to accommodate the committee rooms and offices for the negotiations with Britain, was plunged in gloom. All the suspense, intrigue, hope, and dread which these rooms had witnessed during the ups and downs of the negotiation now gave way to bitterness and anger.

As a result of de Gaulle's action, hundreds of negotiators, from senior cabinet ministers to junior officials, who had been run off their feet working eighteen and twenty hours a day, trying to get through the tangle of dossiers, attending interminable committees, and lobbying other delegations, suddenly found themselves with nothing to do. Politicians with their futures to think of, senior diplomats exasperated by the wasted effort, young enthusiasts furious at being deprived of the exhilarating task of building a new Europe – all shared an appalled sense of anti-climax.

The technicality of the issues involved and the specially-invented

11

jargon in which they were expressed had concealed from outsiders the deep personal involvement of many of the negotiators. They felt the rupture like the death of an old friend.

A few days before, in London, when the negotiations were virtually over and I was preparing to leave for Brussels to report the final round, I had telephoned one of the leading continental negotiators to ask the latest news. In return he asked for a favour: would I bring him the fine and moving photograph the *Observer* had published of Mr Edward Heath, at the moment the news of the rupture had been announced? He wanted it as a memento. That was why, as I drove up on Tuesday afternoon, 29 January, to the ministerial building at No. 2, rue des Quatre Bras, I was clutching Stuart Heydinger's photograph of the Lord Privy Seal, blown up by courtesy of the *Observer* Art Department, showing the usually debonair face lined with grief, as a farewell present to one of the angriest diplomats upstairs.

The last private meeting of Britain and the Six was called to order soon after I arrived, at twenty minutes past four. The atmosphere when it began was already tense. France, at an earlier meeting with the Six, had been bitterly criticized, but it was clear by the time the three British ministers, Mr Heath and Sir Winston Churchill's two sons-in-law (Messrs Sandys and Soames), took their seats, that there was no longer any hope of a last-minute reprieve.

So the speeches began. The ministers spoke not to convince one another but only for the record.

Each of France's five partners reiterated the same conviction: Europe needs Britain, the negotiations should go on. As everybody in that tense room expected, the most brutal denunciation of the French came from the Belgian Foreign Minister, M. Spaak. The quarrel between Spaak, a short, podgy, and naturally pugnacious man, and de Gaulle was an old story, dating back to the time when Spaak was Secretary-General of Nato. Spaak was used to the General's contrariness, but the sudden, brutal press conference was too much. He could not forget how, years before, only his own drive and dynamism had forced the Six into overcoming apparently insurmountable differences, and agreeing on the text of the Rome Treaty. This time, Spaak had cast himself in the role of grand conciliator who, single-handed, would lead Britain into Europe; but the General had frustrated him.

The other ministers present noticed that at his final session Spaak had his discreet Prime Minister at his side. Little had been heard of M. Lefèvre during the months of negotiations, and when he arrived now he modestly introduced himself to the visiting ministers as 'Lefèvre, Prime Minister of Belgium'. The story flying round Brussels that morning had been that the Belgian Cabinet was divided, and that Spaak's fury was not shared by all his colleagues. Certainly the right-wing Catholic party, and some Belgian businessmen, had little use for what they called Spaak's 'tantrums'; many of them were secretly whispering that they were delighted with de Gaulle's decision to keep Britain out. The appearance of Lefèvre was evidently intended to make his Cabinet's position entirely clear, and he sat nodding while Spaak castigated de Gaulle's action as 'brutal', deplored it as a 'defeat for Europe', and accused the French of dishonourably reversing their policies and violating their international agreements.

The Dutch Foreign Minister, M. Luns, spoke more moderately. Though his Government and public were far more unanimously hostile to the rupture than the Belgians, he felt privately that the French had been better friends to Holland than the British. He personally would always be deeply grateful to de Gaulle for having alone been sympathetic to the Dutch in their final stand for New Guinea. Nevertheless, Luns now registered Holland's 'deep disappointment' at the breakdown and expressed the 'grave anxieties' the Dutch felt for the future of Europe and Nato.

Next, Germany. Dr Schroeder, the Foreign Minister of the Federal Republic, had spent most of the previous week in Paris with Chancellor Adenauer – signing the Franco–German treaty of friendship. He thus spoke more in sorrow than in anger. He too was 'deeply disappointed' and shared the general disapproval of the French action. His speech, however, was notable for its restraint.

Then came Italy. The Italian Minister, Signor Emilio Colombo, had distinguished himself during the negotiations by his adroitness in inventing complicated compromises each time the Conference seemed headed for deadlock. Now he seemed discouraged and subdued. There was blame, but no challenge, in his speech.

By the time the sallow sardonic French foreign minister, M. Couve de Murville, took the floor he was strictly on the defensive. He made generous use of the first person singular: 'I believe . . .', 'I wish to assert . . .', 'I find it difficult to understand . . .'. But, everyone knew that the real 'I' was in Paris, inaccessible and intransigent, and that all they were listening to, as Couve spoke, was a faithful recording of his master's voice. 'It's being said here', Couve began, 'that we, the French, are the ones who broke off the negotiations, and must thus take the responsibility for an action which would have grave consequences. In fact, we merely noted that the negotiations had been making no progress since October and simply said it was better to face up to the facts. The facts are that Britain, at present, is not in a state to accept the discipline of the Rome Treaty, notably of carrying out the Community's common agricultural policy. But I must reaffirm that once Britain does feel it can accept all the articles of the Rome Treaty, nothing can prevent it from joining the Common Market. But the onus of proof is on Britain, not on us.'

Nobody took up the challenge. On the eve of this final meeting the Belgians had rushed out a secret conference document, analysing how far Britain had already gone in accepting all the articles of the Rome Treaty. Its authors had worked all night to prepare it, but now nobody even referred to it. As one of the authors remarked: 'What would have been the use? He knew we knew he knew.'

It is now established that Couve de Murville had been unhappy about the General's action, and had warned him in advance that in forcing the rupture he was going to expose his foreign minister to a painful diplomatic drubbing. But when it came, Couve did not flinch: 'Replying to the criticism which is being directed at us on all sides, which alleges that we French have a bias towards a little Europe, I would like to say once again that what we are concerned with is not to promote either a big or a little Europe, but to make sure that the Europe we are about to create is European. This, in our view, is the proper criterion for dealing with the problem of Britain's entry.'

The French Foreign Minister did not attempt to define what he meant by 'European'; nor did he explain why he assumed that Europe would be less European if Britain came in. The answers to these questions were implicit in the General's announcement of the verdict: if Britain came in, de Gaulle had said, the Common Market would have to admit a lot more countries; and in that case 'a colossal Atlantic community would emerge under American dependence and control, which would soon swallow up the European Community'.

Few of the fifty people round the conference table doubted that the General was trying to exclude Britain primarily because she was too tied up with the Americans. But his Minister was right in judging that the less said on this subject the better. For the inescapable consequences of the General's action were to force the other members of the Six to choose between Presidents Kennedy and de Gaulle: and not one of them at this stage could have been relied on to opt for France.

Finally, it was the turn of Britain. Heath's speech was longer than all the others put together. Intent, perhaps, on proving himself as European as the rest, he too avoided mentioning the United States and the Atlantic Community. It was an unusual performance. Heath had never distinguished himself as an orator, and British Members of Parliament liked to say that there was no better soporific in the House of Commons than his weekly progress report on Brussels. Yet he showed himself highly sensitive to this occasion, and 'in offering some comments to my colleagues in this conference, perhaps for the last time', squeezed every drop of sympathy from France's disgruntled partners.

Approving Schroeder's view that Britain's decision to seek entry into Europe 'represented an historic development in British foreign policy', Heath recalled 'the high hopes with which we all set out on this great venture'. Then, after disposing summarily with the remaining items of dispute between the Six and Britain – EFTA, agriculture, tariffs, Commonwealth preferences – saying in each case that agreement had been on the way, he dramatically challenged Couve de Murville's allegation that Britain was not European:

'There have been times in the history of Europe', Heath declared, 'when it has been only too plain how European we are; and there have been many millions of people who have been grateful for it.' Raising his voice slightly he went on: 'The plain fact is that the time has come when the negotiations were for some' [the 'some' was the closest he got to mentioning General de Gaulle] 'too near to success.

'Mr Chairman, as my colleagues have said this afternoon the events of the last few weeks have placed in jeopardy progress towards that true European unity which, I believe, many millions of people desire. But although, as has just been said, this is a sad moment for European unity, I should like straightaway to say one thing. We told you, at the very beginning of these negotiations, that we wanted to go forward with you in the building of a new Europe. Our words were very carefully weighed. They remain true today. We have been encouraged by the upsurge of support for the fullest British participation in a united Europe which has been demonstrated in so many quarters in these recent weeks.

'And so I would say to my colleagues: they should have no fear. We in Britain are not going to turn our backs on the mainland of Europe or on the countries of the Community. We are a part of Europe; by geography, tradition, history, culture, and civilization. We shall continue to work with all our friends in Europe for the true unity and strength of this continent.'

This unambiguous pledge provided a final release for pent-up emotions. The eyes of at least three distinguished listeners, including a commissioner of the Common Market Executive, were seen to glisten, and the simultaneous-interpreter-girls discreetly took hankies out of their bags. For the first time in history, an international economic negotiation was literally ending in tears.

The Belgian Chairman, M. Henri Fayat, wound it up: 'I much regret that in the present circumstances the Six find themselves prevented from continuing negotiations. I therefore declare the seventeenth meeting of this Conference concluded.'

The ministers lined up to shake hands with Heath and to congratulate him on what he had said – a gesture mainly intended to annoy the French. As everybody clustered around the blue-eyed hero of the hour, Couve de Murville stood to one side with a grim smile, showing no sign that he ever wanted to talk to any of them again. It was the General's will.

In Paris, meanwhile, at the very time the conference was breaking up, General de Gaulle was sitting in a private office at the Élysée, taking tea with his old friend, the bearded and affable M. Serge Vinogradoff, Ambassador of the Soviet Union. They were old acquaintances: at a period when most of the foreign diplomatic corps in Paris were breathlessly running round cultivating the changing politicians of the Fourth Republic, M. Vinogradoff had made it a regular practice to call at Colombey-les-deux-Églises, the village where the General was then completing his memoirs and preparing his return.

In Washington and London, word of this tea-time encounter sent a shudder down eminent spines. As soon as the news of the General's rupture of the Common Market negotiations had come through, it had been feared both in Whitehall and in Washington that he would follow his rebuff of the West with some move towards the East. The British Prime Minister himself did not altogether exclude the possibility that the General was now summoning his Soviet friend to suggest a meeting with Mr Khrushchev. This at least would have been one way for the General to demonstrate his indifference to the strictures coming out of Brussels.

Quietly and efficiently the Quai d'Orsay killed the rumour. Key journalists were taken aside and told that M. Vinogradoff had called on the General at his own request; far from giving him a Russian hug, he wanted only to register Soviet disapproval of the new Franco–German Treaty; the synchronization of the tea-party and the Brussels rupture was merely an unfortunate coincidence.

But was it? A few days later the Russians took, for them, the quite unusual step of shedding a little light on their own diplomatic moves. A statement from the Soviet Embassy in Paris confirmed that M. Vinogradoff had indeed wished to register Soviet objection to the Treaty, but he would have been quite prepared to deliver this message to the Foreign Ministry; instead, he had been directed to call at the Élysée by the personal invitation of General de Gaulle. None of this caused much disturbance among the people of Paris.

As a newspaper vendor commented: '*Le Général fait encore son cinéma. . . .*' But elsewhere de Gaulle's activities filled those who worry about such things with a sudden cold alarm. The whole structure of Western alliances, built up with such labour since the end of the Second World War, seemed to be trembling.

CHAPTER TWO

DE GAULLE: MAN AND MONARCH

As that bleak and snow-bound January came to an end, there seemed to be only one topic in the alarmed embassies and foreign offices of the West: de Gaulle. Suddenly everyone seemed to realize that they knew much less about this strange man than they had assumed. What was he up to? What stakes was he playing for? Could he really be preparing to demolish the alliances of the West, and if so, would it be only for personal ambition or with some secret grand design? What kind of man was de Gaulle?

Few people can have studied the de Gaulle phenomenon with more attention than the General himself. He is that rare specimen: a man who invented his own character. He can almost be seen staggering under the weight of a legendary superman whom he himself created for the glory of France and de Gaulle.

Is there still, hidden somewhere inside this incredible artefact, a real person with pity for his fellow men, an occasional urge for pleasure, and a mortal's fear of death? No one will ever know. The man whom the President of France so often refers to in the third person, whose place in history (as he once told Duff Cooper) he takes a little time off each day to examine, and who corresponds so neatly with his own youthful vision of the hero-martyr-patriot – this is the only de Gaulle the world will be allowed to see.

It is sometimes supposed that this archaic figure (is it by chance that his presidential office in the Élysée is decorated by a classical tapestry of Don Quixote?), brought up as he was in a highly conventional army family, was no more than a small-town provincial officer without any real contact with the intellectual ferment of his time. On the contrary, though it is true that his philosophical curiosity was satisfied early in life, and that he rarely absorbs ideas produced after the First World War, he comes from a distinguished and intellectually eminent family, with judges, historians, teachers, and writers among his forebears.

The de Gaulles were never near the top of the aristocratic pyramid, but claim enough pedigree to allow de Gaulle, after the Common Market rupture, to tell an African dignitary that this was not the first time his family had come to grips with the English. According to the family legend there was a Sir Jehan de Gaulle leading an archery attack of four hundred men on the morning of 25 October 1415 at the Battle of Agincourt.

The family has been in Paris since the eighteenth century but comes from Flanders. Through several generations de Gaulles, including the General's own father, found themselves attracted to another respectable Flemish family, the Maillots. Modern psychiatrists deny there is any proven link between interbreeding and degeneracy, although some historians have been inclined to see in the frequent de Gaulle–Maillot intermarriages the origin of a streak of misfortune which has dogged the family. One of de Gaulle's own brothers was a paralytic and one of his three children was mentally defective and died before she was twenty-one.

As a boy Charles grew too fast. His height and conspicuous but unprepossessing appearance earned him the nickname 'the asparagus' and may have helped to isolate him from other children. The peculiar trait of friendlessness, a necessity of which he was to make a virtue, certainly began in his earliest youth. It was in this enforced isolation that he first pondered the destiny of great men whose exceptional qualities separate them from their fellows. It is possible, of course, that had he not been brought up in an austere, buttoned-up home by a highly conventional family his remarkable qualities – a prodigious memory, outstanding skills as logician and writer, physical and moral bravery, thrust, vision, and enterprise – might have been directed towards a less frenetically lonely existence. As it was, the idea of a superman personifying the nation's destiny occupied his mind from an early age.

The mystique of the nation-state as the supreme repository of human endeavour, and its counterpart, the need for its embodiment in a single leader, was not an idea invented by the General. He grew up when jingoism was at its zenith and made respectable by highsounding philosophical doctrines. In the words of his wartime Minister of the Interior, Emmanual d'Astier, whose brief biography of the General is perhaps the best, de Gaulle 'was to make of Nietzsche, Charles Maurras, and Machiavelli a very personal salad'.

There is obviously a good deal of Nietzsche in the superman de Gaulle created and became. Yet his orthodox Catholic upbringing and convictions always made it impossible for him to accept the cult of physical violence and totalitarianism adopted by other Nietzsche disciples. His first book, *Discord among our Enemies*, written partly during his two years as a German prisoner-of-war and published in 1924, attributed the defeat of the German leaders to their acceptance of Nietzsche's theories of an élite to whom everything – 'violence, passions, personal ambition' – is allowed. De Gaulle instead counselled moderation and restraint, praising the perfections of a French garden with its geometric harmonies and '*le sens de l'équilibre, du possible, de la mesure*'.

It was already plain that the arbitrary tyranny of the Nazis would repel him: he was never among those French right-wingers who, in the thirties, were sucked into the extremist factions. Charges of 'Fascism' levelled against him both during the war and more recently have always been wholly unjust.

His association with Charles Maurras, the second ingredient of his salad, was more complicated. He certainly owed more to the French philosopher of absolutism, the men who castigated the Republic as '*la gueuse*' (the harlot), than to any other thinker. From Maurras he took the idea of the '*pays réel*', to which patriotism is due, as a separate phenomenon from the '*pays légal*', the country expressed in its existing institutions. In the famous first sentence of his *Memoirs* – '*Toute ma vie je me suis fait une certaine idée de la France*' – he is manifestly talking of the *pays réel*: an infinite splendour, quite detached from the *pays légal*, the old Third Republic he despised.

Also from Maurras comes the deep monarchial strain in de Gaulle's thinking: the idea of the chief, above party politics, embodying the whole nation. The General remains to this day convinced that the French people, despite their revolutions and reigns of terror, are basically monarchist, and that they respond best not to the tyranny of a demagogue who depends on plebiscites and passion, but to the staid control of a monarch whom they feel incarnates their collective personality. Looking back on June

1940, de Gaulle was able to write: '*En ce moment, le pire de son histoire, c'était à moi d'assumer la France*' – it was my task, at this moment, the worst in her history, to take France over. Since then, the General has thought of himself as a reigning monarch. The Fourth Republic was endorsed many times over by the French electorate, but for de Gaulle it was always a régime of usurpers until, in May 1958, Charles was restored to his throne.

Yet, though mentally attuned to Maurras, de Gaulle was too good a Catholic to support him once his totalitarian views brought him into collision with the Vatican. Indeed there is only one pre-war incident on record when the future general did get himself involved in a political fight. This was when he accepted an invitation from the intellectual wing of the Maurras Movement, the Cercle Fustel de Coulange, to repeat, in a Sorbonne lecture-hall, talks on the role of the army which he had first delivered at the War College. In glorifying '*l'esprit militaire*' as vital to the nation, de Gaulle offended the pacifist and left-wing leanings of a large part of the student body. Charles Cattoui, the General's preferred biographer, writes: 'The success of these talks produced unfortunate repercussions and, as a result of disturbances and interruptions, the lectures had to be suspended.'

It was in 1932, the year of his most famous book, *Fil de l'Épée*, that de Gaulle revealed the third, Machiavellian ingredient of his salad: the ideal of a prince who is free from the normal bonds of conscience and who requires, in that unforgettable Gaullist phrase, '*une forte dose d'égoïsme, d'orgueil, de dureté, et de ruse*'. All these four qualities have been developed to their limits by the General, during his two spells of power.

Égoïsme: The '*Moi, Général de Gaulle*' (first introduced to France by the B.B.C. during the war) is, in the General's view, the incarnation of France, which is the most important country of the most important continent in the world. Not for de Gaulle the 'cowardly modesty' he notes in lesser men. The General indeed has never hesitated to compare himself with the greatest figures of French history – Joan of Arc, Louis XIV, Napoleon, Clemenceau – unperturbed by the sardonic laughter evoked by these comparisons, especially the first. Once when some misguided visitors to the Élysée dared to refer to the General's predecessors, thinking of the former occupants of the presidential palace, he cut in: '*Messieurs, sachez que de Gaulle n'a pas de prédécesseurs!*' On one of his tours of the French provinces local notabilities told him that as long as he was their leader, they had nothing to fear: but what would come after? 'France,' they were told, 'must find another de Gaulle.' It is precisely this egoism which has been such a boon to satirists and mimics the world over. It would be a poor dinner party in Paris these days if none of the guests was capable of raising a laugh by a recognizable imitation of the 'supreme guide'.

Orgueil: The General's pride shows itself in a most inconvenient form, in his daily conduct of state business. He never asks to see anyone. If anyone wishes to see him, they may seek an audience. The result is that some very important Frenchmen, politicians, businessmen, labour leaders, have never been admitted to the Élysée at all.

The General is too proud to ask for what he wants. Everyone knows how strongly he feels that France must have its own nuclear striking force. He is not unnaturally resentful that nuclear secrets, shared by the United States and Britain, and certainly known to the Russians, are withheld from France. Millions of pounds and years of research are today being wasted by the French Treasury while France repeats the whole process of nuclear research. It is fairly clear in retrospect, and it is confirmed by senior members of the Élysée staff, that what the General wanted from the British during recent European discussions was an offer of nuclear partnership which would have allowed the two countries to share their knowledge and work together. Whether or not this was the best way of serving Western interests, the idea would certainly have evoked considerable sympathy from the British Government, which shared the General's own belief in a national nuclear deterrent. There is reason to believe that if he had come forward with a specific proposal, even if it had involved renegotiating Britain's agreements with the United States, it would have received the Prime Minister's careful attention. The General, however, felt he must not demean himself by indicating what he wanted.

Dureté: Anyone who works closely with the General is always astonished by his indifference to the well-being of even his most fervent supporters. He has a manifest contempt for his own Cabinet

23

ministers: they can be seen squirming with embarrassment over decisions he has taken without asking their advice and has then left them to carry out. Michel Debré, who, in the days of Gaullist opposition, frequently and publicly declared that any politician who separated Algeria from France would be guilty of high treason, was Prime Minister when the General decided to accept the rebel Algerian demand for total independence. Debré entreated the General to let him resign. 'No, Debré,' the General is reported to have said. 'I need you.' Later, when Debré was not needed any more, he was dismissed without even the support he required to preserve his seat in Parliament, which he accordingly lost at the next general election.

Again, it was Couve de Murville, a diplomatist whose whole training inclined him towards manoeuvre and manipulation, who was suddenly given the task of disrupting the Brussels negotiations. A current joke in Paris describes a high-level dinner party where everybody is deploring the alarming state of France's international relations, upon which M. Couve cuts in to observe 'Ah! If only I were Foreign Minister!'

The General is beyond the reach of sentiment. During the long Algerian war the French Army and police, both in Metropolitan France and Algeria, made extensive use of torture to extract information, mostly from civilians, often from women. These methods began under the Fourth Republic, but when the General took over, his minister, André Malraux, said they would have to stop. Yet, despite violent protests (in which a niece of the General played a conspicuous part), the use of torture continued, and even increased, as the war dragged on. A group of objectors, mainly Catholics with special access to the Élysée, decided to ask the General to intervene. They chose as their spokesman a well-known French writer, a man who had himself suffered in Nazi concentration camps. The General received him and listened while he listed the evidence of what was happening and protested that these methods would ruin future relations between France and Algeria. Then the General interrupted. '*Le sang*', he said, '*sèche vite*' (blood dries quickly).

Certainly de Gaulle himself has no time for pity. The explosion of an atom bomb over Hiroshima, for instance, caused many varied reactions. Some felt that it was an intrinsically evil act. Others believed that it was justified since it shortened the war. De Gaulle heard the news with absolute calm: his only comment was that this would surely open the way for France to regain Indo-China. Sixteen years later, when France exploded its own first nuclear bomb, he sent the officers concerned one of the merriest messages this usually melancholy man has ever penned: 'Hurrah for France! From this day she is stronger and prouder . . .'.

Ruse: The most conspicuous case of cunning and stealth in modern history is the story of how the General, after seeing his predecessors overthrown for allegedly contemplating peace negotiations in Algeria, took over power and gradually got the Army and the country to give the rebels everything they had ever been fighting for.

Contrary to a myth cultivated by the Gaullists, the General had not always believed in the independence of France's overseas possessions. He was himself in power in May 1945 when the first nationalist uprising in Algeria was suppressed. Two years after the event, French investigators revealed that some fifteen thousand Arab lives had been lost; a French Army general, reporting to the Senate on the events, said: 'We regret having to say that groups of armed settlers were arrogating themselves the right to pass judgement and to execute. The government of the time [de Gaulle] by failing to punish these actions, was guilty of denying justice and truth to the people for whom it was responsible.'

Reporting many years later on the seven-year Algerian war of independence, a Swiss journalist, Charles-Henri Favrod, wrote: 'All the nationalists I met agreed on one thing: the revolution of 1954 (the year of the outbreak of the war which ended France's rule) was predetermined by the events of 1945. All the Nationalists I met at Cairo, Rome, Tunis, Bonn, Geneva, gave me hair-raising accounts of the massacres of those days and nights.'

But during his long retirement at Colombey the General had come to terms with the idea that French withdrawal from Algeria was inevitable. A few weeks before returning to power in 1958 he received at his country home his wartime economic adviser, Georges Boris (uncle of the senior foreign office official, Olivier

Wormser who was later to lead the French team in the Common Market negotiations with Britain), and told him that Algeria was moving inevitably towards independence. Back in office, de Gaulle's first task was to ensure Army loyalty; and soon he was holding wide his arms in Algeria and proclaiming: '*Je vous ai compris!*' to the cheering French settlers, who not unnaturally assumed he was going to be on their side. He subsequently offered '*la solution la plus française*', which most people assumed meant keeping Algeria French (his supporters later pointed out that freedom and national independence were very French concepts).

Thus he played along the Army with a string of ambiguities, leaving everyone uncertain of his intentions. In May 1960 he visited Army camps dotted around Algeria and dined at the officers' messes. He told them that Algerian independence was 'absurd' and 'unthinkable', and the Algerians must become 'fully-fledged Frenchmen' (*français à part entière*). A year later he was still saying he would never discuss Algeria's future with cut-throats and rebels.

The Army were not the only ones whom de Gaulle deceived. While the war dragged on it remained official French policy to secure Moslem cooperation; thus hundreds of thousands of Moslems, needing food and shelter, and apparently trusting the French promise that any new régime would give them a share in the country's political life, accepted French protection.

I cannot myself forget long arguments I used to have with a parachutist officer, Commander Saint-Marc, on the morality and wisdom of the integrationist policy by which the Army hoped to make Algerians full French citizens. Saint-Marc had himself fought in Indo-China and was appalled at having left so many Vietnamese who had worked with the French to be rounded up, mutilated, and killed by triumphant nationalists. Never again! he used to say – determined that in Algeria the Army would stay on and create a new modern state where the people would be safe, social justice would be done, and France would use its resources and skill to combat hunger, illiteracy, and unemployment.

Then, suddenly, the General agreed to hand over the whole of Algeria to the F.L.N. Great concern has often and rightly been expressed at the U.N. and elsewhere over the appallingly high casualties among the Arab nationalists during the seven terrible years of war. But little is ever said by either side of the many thousands of friends of France who have subsequently died because they believed de Gaulle's promises. As for Saint-Marc, he is today in prison, charged with mutiny.

But Machiavelli was right: the Prince, after double-crossing everyone, was stronger at home and abroad than ever before.

CHAPTER THREE

DE GAULLE: ANGLO-SAXON ATTITUDES

IT is one of the great paradoxes of contemporary history that it was an Englishman who first enabled the General to exercise those prince-like qualities that were to cause Britain so much trouble. Fortunately, in the difficult days after the rupture at Brussels, nobody was tactless enough to ask the classical question: '*Qui t'a fait roi?*' De Gaulle's own answer would have been 'Providence'; but the truth is that he was installed on the Thames Embankment as leader of the fighting French by Winston Churchill, then Prime Minister of England – mainly because nobody more eminent turned up.

It was on Monday 17 June 1940 that de Gaulle was flown to England in an R.A.F. fighter aircraft with no more than a few thousand pounds from the secret service fund of his Prime Minister, Paul Reynaud. The British promptly gave him offices, money, and (most important of all) radio facilities, to stimulate as many Frenchmen as possible to go on with the war. Thereafter, with extraordinary speed and dexterity, de Gaulle asserted himself as leader of the Fighting French. Before long his name became associated in Metropolitan France with the struggle for national liberation, and he acquired a status and authority independent of his British paymasters.

Ten days after his arrival in Britain he received a letter from M. Jean Monnet, who was also then in London: 'You are wrong', said M. Monnet, 'to form an organization which might appear in France as under British protection. I fully share your wish to prevent France from abandoning the struggle. But it is not from London that the effort of resurrection can begin.'

But the General did not need to be reminded that he must on no account appear to the French as England's puppet. Being the *enfant terrible* among the crowd of exiled dignitaries became for him an imperative daily duty. Churchill was later to recall that he had many crosses to bear during the war, but the heaviest of all was the Cross of Lorraine, the Gaullist emblem. Nobody was prouder of this than General de Gaulle. Describing his farewell, at the end of the war, to the then Foreign Minister, Anthony Eden, he recalls this final and, he assures us, good-humoured exchange:

EDEN: Do you know you caused us more trouble than all our other European allies put together?
DE GAULLE: I don't doubt it. France is a great power.

Throughout the Second World War, the General had two principal aims: first, to prepare for the peaceful takeover of a France ready to assume her place as one of the world's great powers; and second, to preserve the French Empire. His *Memoirs*, indeed, deal in such detail with the jostlings between himself and the Western Allies that when he sent a complimentary copy of his book to a French political leader, P.-H. Teitgen, who had himself fought in the French Resistance, Teitgen thanked him, declared the *Memoirs* a splendid work, and added that somehow he and the General did not seem to have been fighting the same war.

Accepting, as his over-riding war-aim, the revival of France as a great power, the General had little sympathy with, or even grasp of, the concept of a collective Allied purpose: to smash Nazism and restore European democracy. Even now, the General looks back on the last war in purely national and not in the least in ideological terms. During his last visit to Germany, he spoke publicly of the terrible mistake the two countries had twice committed in fighting each other 'because an arch-duke was dead or someone had invaded Danzig'.

At the beginning of the war, the word 'democratic' itself was suspect to the General. The editor of the wartime daily, *France*, the French newspaper, financed by the British Ministry of Information for the wartime colony in London, recalls inviting the General to celebrate the first number. The next morning the General's aide-de-camp telephoned to say that the General approved of the contents of the paper, but was doubtful about the three words under the masthead. Didn't they think that '*Liberté, Égalité, Fraternité*' might divide the French?

The General's failure to concede that Britain and France were fighting a common battle caused him, from the start, to insist on sole control of Resistance activities inside France. These were to be directed not only against the Germans, but also in preparing a Gaullist takeover after liberation. Many Frenchmen who thought they were doing their patriotic duty by working with British intelligence networks discovered when they got to London that the General regarded them as no better than mercenaries. De Gaulle recalls in his *Memoirs* that he did his best to remind Frenchmen 'of their moral and legal obligation not to place themselves in the service of a foreign power'.

De Gaulle was not a man to forget: touring the provinces after the Liberation, he made a practice of refusing to shake hands with any French or British officers whose contribution to the war effort, however heroic, had been made on French soil under any authority but his own.

In the struggle to preserve the French Empire, the biggest explosion was over Syria and the Lebanon. On no fewer than three occasions the General, living on British soil and on British money, sent stern ultimatums to the British Government, warning them that unless they recognized French authority, he would break off relations with them – war or no war. Both he and the British agreed that the Vichy authorities had to be evicted from the Middle East lest they handed it over to Germany. But whereas the British encouraged Arab nationalism against Vichy, de Gaulle thought that he himself should be Vichy's successor. He was unshakeably convinced that all the British talk of Arab nationalism was merely a device for replacing French by British influence. In 1941 he privately bemoaned the weakness of his devoted representative in the Middle East, General Georges Catroux, because he 'was particularly slow in fathoming the full depth of the malevolence of British intentions. . . .'

At first there was not much de Gaulle could do, except threaten. Then, on 2 June 1942, as we now know from the Soviet Foreign Ministry's publication in 1959 of their wartime correspondence on France, he made his first – though certainly not his last – bid for Soviet support against the British and Americans. In a brief despatch, the Soviet Ambassador to the Allied Governments in London, Bogomolov, reported to Molotov, then Soviet Foreign

Minister, that General de Gaulle had come to see him. 'De Gaulle said that the Americans were preparing to seize Dakar and the British were planning to take over Algeria with no regard for France. He asked whether we would be willing to receive the Free French headquarters and their forces in the Soviet Union.' Ten days later Moscow received a second despatch. The General's adviser on foreign affairs, M. Dejean, had called on Bogomolov to urge him not to exaggerate the differences between the Western Allies, and to say that there was no need at this time to contemplate the removal of the Free French from London.

It has often been suggested on the basis of his wartime and subsequent behaviour that the General is intrinsically anglophobe. It is true that he was educated at St-Cyr before the First World War, when the dominant passion in France was still the shame of Fashoda, after the ignominious expulsion of the French by the British. Anglophobia was certainly an integral part of the Maurrasien tradition.

But in his book *The Army of the Future*, published in 1934, de Gaulle wrote:

After many conflicts, London and Paris have settled their political differences. So long as the French accept British maritime supremacy and avoid mentioning certain Norman islands, and as long as France submits to certain forms of supervision, we can count on England's neutrality, jealous of us in our time of prosperity but well disposed during our misfortunes, up to a point which might produce an alliance based on mutual interests.

(This book was translated into English and rushed out by Hutchinson at the beginning of the war; but in this edition the sentence quoted above is modestly abbreviated to read: 'In return for the acknowledgement of British maritime supremacy, we can count on English neutrality, and may turn that neutrality into an alliance for mutual interest.')

Perhaps one of de Gaulle's senior civil servants was near the truth when he denied that the General was anglophobe and suggested instead that he was schizophrenic about England: fearing and admiring at the same time. It is certainly true that de Gaulle throughout the war assumed Britain was trying to take advantage of French weakness. But believing as he does that jungle law must exist between all nation-states, he privately acknowledged that he would have done the same to Britain if their positions had been the other way round. To him, it was '*la bonne guerre*'. Similarly today, when Britain appears economically and diplomatically vulnerable, he sees nothing wrong in trying to strengthen France at Britain's expense.

Basically, de Gaulle still believes that Britain and France are the greatest and oldest civilizations in the world. In one of his earlier works he went so far as to claim that the French Army founded British greatness. He explained that 'Great Britain was conquered by men of our country, from whom sprang the British aristocracy, the force and grandeur of England. . . .' For a traditionalist and a monarchist like de Gaulle there is a great deal in Britain to admire. Contrary to what most people thought at the time, those close to him are convinced that the effusive speech he made at Westminster during his 1960 state visit to London was a genuine expression of his views: 'Which people know better than the French and English that nothing can save the world if not the qualities in which they, above all other nations, excel: wisdom and firmness.'

But if the General fundamentally sees Britain as an esteemed and equal rival, his approach to the United States is, on the contrary, tinged with antipathy and fear. He often expatiates in private on America's lack of nationhood and absence of historic tradition, and remains obsessed by the conviction that this upstart country, by the sheer force of its industrial might, may eliminate France permanently from the big-power group.

His anti-Americanism is partly temperamental. The General, with his austere Jansenist background and his rigid code of manners, simply rejects the pursuit of happiness as a tolerable human objective.

This natural repulsion was increased by the heavy-handed way in which President Roosevelt tried to remove him from the wartime leadership of the French. Until the Americans came into the war, they preserved diplomatic relations with Vichy; afterwards, Roosevelt's advisers continued to believe that the Vichy régime could not only survive the peace but would be preferable to a Gaullist interregnum. In North Africa the Americans managed to preserve Vichy law and personnel long after all the main resistance movements in France had accepted the leadership of de Gaulle. Refusing to admit this proof that de Gaulle had thereby acquired all the backing he needed to preserve the integrity of France, and avoid civil war or a communist takeover after liberation, the Americans stolidly went on training their own and British officers to administer France. They even printed their own currency, as though they could treat France, once they got there, as enemy territory. The greatest British expert on French politics, Professor D. W. Brogan, recalls that the silliest of his wartime assignments was teaching selected British and American officers how to govern France.

The General was certainly right in believing that Roosevelt thought France was finished, and that the sooner she liquidated her overseas empire the better. He was wrong, however, in attributing Roosevelt's dislike and suspicion of himself, which was real, personal, and persistent, to a secret policy for demoting France. Roosevelt in fact regarded France's fall from the ranks of the great powers as an ineluctable result of the 1940 defeat.

This was why Roosevelt was unwilling to admit de Gaulle to the allied conference at Yalta in 1945, where Europe and the Far East were discussed between himself, Stalin, and Churchill. On his way home, Roosevelt did indeed invite de Gaulle to call on him at Algiers. In his *Memoirs* the General described how preposterous it was for the President to presume to invite the head of the French State to meet him on French territory after disposing of Europe in France's absence. What he does not say, though it can be revealed now, is that the Americans had made an unofficial approach to him beforehand, and only made their invitation public when they were told that de Gaulle would come. The General wanted the pleasure of publicly humiliating the leader of the world's strongest power.

From the very beginning until the fateful January 1963 press conference, de Gaulle's most serious dispute with the British has been that, in his deep and irreconcilable struggle with the Americans, the British could always be relied upon to take the American side. The worst wartime dramas were precisely on this issue. (The General himself later brought back into use the epithet

'Anglo-Saxon', which had originally been popularized by the Quisling press and radio during the war – often linked with the other pejorative terms, Communist and Jew.)

Thus, the worst Churchill–de Gaulle collision, in the mid-summer of 1943, was caused by the Americans supporting General Giraud as the only possible commander-in-chief of French troops in North Africa. Suddenly, in June 1943, de Gaulle, who had been working with Giraud in the French National Committee, sent him an ultimatum that unless he got out, de Gaulle himself would withdraw. Mr Harold Macmillan, in those days political adviser at Eisenhower's Algiers headquarters, relayed the news to Churchill. 'You are quite right to play for time', Churchill replied, 'and let de Gaulle have every chance to come to his senses and realize the forces around him.' Churchill referred Macmillan to St Matthew, Chapter 7, verse 16: 'Beware of False prophets which come to you in sheep's clothing but inwardly are ravening wolves. By their fruits ye shall know them. . . .' Macmillan, who was perhaps a better friend of de Gaulle than the General realized, replied: 'Doing my best. See Revelation 2, verses 2–5.' ('I know thy works and thy toil and patience, and that thou canst not bear evil men . . . but I have this against thee, that thou didst leave thy first love.')

We shall not know precisely Macmillan's role at Eisenhower's Headquarters until he gives us his own account, but there is reason to believe that each time Roosevelt ordered Eisenhower to get rid of de Gaulle, Macmillan did his best to get Eisenhower to procrastinate. But Macmillan never allowed the French to detect any Anglo–American split. A few months earlier, on 17 March, acting on Anglo–American instructions, Macmillan had called in one of de Gaulle's aides and urged him to persuade the General to rally his forces around Giraud. According to de Gaulle's account, when the unfortunate aide expressed doubts about whether this could be done, Macmillan shouted: 'If General de Gaulle refuses the hand stretched out towards him, let him know that Britain and the United States will abandon him completely – and he will be nothing any more!'

By that mid summer, Churchill was seriously considering scuttling de Gaulle. After Macmillan's message about the General's June ultimatum, Churchill took the unusual step of personally

34

preparing an anti-Gaullist press directive to soften public opinion in case of rupture. This directive was discussed between the Minister of Information, Brendan Bracken, and British and American journalists in London, and then sent to the State Department in Washington which leaked the text to the *Washington Post*. The terms were extremely strong: Churchill stated that de Gaulle 'can no longer be considered a reliable friend of Britain'; accused him of having tried to split Great Britain and the United States; claimed that he had created friction between the British and French in Syria; and described him as having 'Fascist and dictatorial tendencies'.

Back in Algiers, the General quietly ignored the hubbub. Instead he went on with his task of building up the links with the French underground, which were eventually to carry him un-opposed to power. Giraud, little by little, was squeezed out; and as the focus of Allied attention swung from Africa to Europe, America's protégé politically ceased to exist.

Even then the General's troubles were not over. On the eve of D-Day, he once again found Churchill taking the Americans' side. In future years, and again in January 1963, he was often to recall that when final preparations for the Normandy landings were under way, of which the General had not yet been told, Allied intelligence, as part of its security measures, interrupted his secret communications between Algiers and London. He retaliated immediately: in the last weeks before the invasion French officers were forbidden to have any dealings at all with the Allied High Command.

Then on 3 June, three days before D-Day, de Gaulle was flown back to London in a British plane. Next morning he saw both Churchill and Eisenhower. The British Prime Minister received him in a railway coach not far from Eisenhower's headquarters at Widewing, a secret camp in the woods near Portsmouth. Churchill asked de Gaulle to broadcast with other Allied leaders on D-Day, calling on the French to support the Allies; he was also asked to assign French liaison officers to accompany the Anglo–American invasion forces. De Gaulle, however, had discovered that Eisenhower in *his* broadcast proposed to tell the French people that they would be free after the war to select their own government. De Gaulle saw this as a denial of authority to the Free French – and categorically refused both Churchill's requests. After lunch Churchill took him to see Eisenhower and he was shown the offending script. He was adamant. In the end only a small batch of Free French officers accompanied the Allied invasion, and de Gaulle's address to the French nation was delivered not with other allied leaders, in the original programme, but several hours later – this freed him from in any sense endorsing the American line.

When the General left Eisenhower he was in such an exalted state of indignation that he refused even the hospitality of Churchill's car back to London, let alone the Prime Minister's invitation to dinner. On the last day before the invasion Churchill got so fed up that he went so far as to dictate, though not to send off, a letter to de Gaulle, threatening to send him back to Algiers and denounce him for refusing to associate himself with France's liberation.

Looking back at that climax of the war, on which the future of Europe and the lives of millions depended, this personal bickering seems infinitely absurd. But for de Gaulle, living up to his legendary personage, the style of his re-entry into France was vital. Everything he had achieved up to then would be lost, he thought, if France were taken over at the moment of liberation by the Allied powers. And he got his way: Eisenhower delivered his broadcast despite de Gaulle's objections; but the Gaullists had the apparatus in France ready for the takeover. The plans for an Allied military government were quietly scrapped.

Immediately after D-Day the Americans even refused to allow de Gaulle to go back to France. Lord Boothby, who was then an M.P., has recently revealed that he had obtained the permission of the Speaker to move an adjournment on 'a definite matter of public interest, namely the refusal of Allied Headquarters to allow General de Gaulle to land on the shores of France'. Lord Boothby says that Churchill told him he would not authorize a public debate and the motion was consequently withdrawn.

A few days later the General did get permission for a visit to the Normandy beachhead. His first act, characteristically, was to go directly to the nearest Prefecture to install his own nominees. He summarily rejected an invitation to lunch at the Allies' head-quarters at Bayeux: 'I didn't come back to France', he said 'to lunch with General Montgomery'. Back in Paris his quarrels with the Allies continued: when it had been agreed with difficulty (and thanks mainly to Churchill) that the French would be given a zone of occupation in Germany, de Gaulle tried hard to grasp as big a slab of territory as he could. Former President Truman has recently recalled how he personally ordered American supplies to be withheld from Free French Forces until General de Gaulle could be forced to get his troops out of Stuttgart, which had been allocated to the Americans.

De Gaulle has never rid himself of his antipathy for the Americans. Still, he is not a man to allow his personal feelings to interfere with what he judges to be politically necessary. There have been several times, since the end of the war, when he has felt that France's greatness, even its survival, has depended on working on the American side in the Cold War. Even though today he dislikes American meddling in Europe, he would certainly be the first to deplore the withdrawal of the American nuclear umbrella before he has achieved his ambition of building a strong Western Europe under French leadership, which can provide its own military protection.

Again, it is now known that in the years immediately after the war the General was convinced that an East–West conflict was imminent, but it never crossed his mind that he could be other than on the Western side. There would be little room for a resurrected France, still less for her monarch, if the Communists took over. After his resignation in 1946, he formed a patriotic political move-ment – *la Rassemblement du Peuple Français* – which was far more militantly anti-communist than the Government. I remember being told at the time by André Malraux, then his principal lieutenant, of de Gaulle's conviction that when the conflict began the French communists would seize Paris and that the R.P.F. would have to be ready to build resistance in other parts of France, with de Gaulle again in his Joan of Arc role, personifying resistance. The Americans themselves, with Roosevelt's death, had forgotten their old quarrels; and they were far from uninterested in the General's new anti-communist front. The R.P.F. – it can now be stated with certainty – could never have managed their great propaganda drive without American secret service funds.

More recently, as the risk of war has receded and the nuclear stalemate has given lesser powers more freedom of action, the General has been quick to resume what he judges to be his historic task: the promotion of French national grandeur by the elimination of American control. This is the reason for the objection to placing French forces under American command and to his frequent comparisons of the Nato concept of 'integration' with Soviet satellization of Eastern Europe.

In the General's view, the present outlook is for peace, and he is determined to be the subject, not the object, of any East–West bargain on the future of Europe.

As de Gaulle grows older, his bias against the United States has increasingly conditioned his behaviour. While most of Western Europe has cheered the end of American isolation and its full commitment to European defence and to transatlantic partnership, the General has detected sinister Yankee designs to capture and cow the great nations of Europe.

This attitude explains his recent alarm over American investments in France, although these account for less than half the proportion of the Gross National Product owned by Americans in Germany or Britain.

Hence, too, his hostility to President Kennedy's plans for increasing transatlantic trade.

'Can it really be,' I once asked one of his cabinet ministers, 'that the General suspects that the Kennedy Trade Expansion Act is an American takeover bid for western Europe?'

'It's not a suspicion,' the minister replied. 'It's a certainty.'

CHAPTER FOUR

NEW NOTIONS OF EUROPE

WHEN Europeans stopped killing each other at the end of the war, everyone declared themselves in favour of European union. It was unanimous: like being against sin.

It soon became clear, however, that the words 'European' and 'union' were being used by different people to mean different things. For de Gaulle, who felt he had fought the whole war almost single-handed against Anglo-Saxon hegemony, the attraction of uniting Europe was to create a new centre of power to tilt the balance.

Even before the German collapse, the General had been dreaming of a new European cadre for a resurrected France. Early in 1944 in Algeria some of his advisers had been examining the usefulness of working out joint development plans with Belgium and Holland once the war was over. The idea was put to de Gaulle, who astonished his ministers by saying that both for defence and for economic well-being France needed a wider base than her own frontiers. But he felt that her little Northern neighbours hardly sufficed. As he, de Gaulle, saw it, Italy, Portugal, and Spain – all presumably freed after the war from Fascism – would be France's proper partners. The French, in the name of this wider community, could then demand control over the Rhineland and the Ruhr, to be managed in Europe's collective interest. Only thus, the General thought, could France resist Anglo–American superiority. It was only after leaving de Gaulle that it occurred to one of his ministers that the General had spontaneously redrawn the contours of Napoleon's empire.

The last volume of the General's *Memoirs*, published in 1959, reveals similar aspirations. Describing the situation in 1944, when he returned to Paris after the war, the General says that antagonism between Russia and the U.S.A. 'offered France miraculously exceptional chances of action. It seemed that this new period now beginning might allow me to carry through the vast plans I had formed for my country'. He then describes his plan:

Ensure security by preventing the rebirth of a new Reich. Maintain contacts with both East and West, if necessary making alliances on either side without ever accepting any kind of dependence. . . . Lead the states bordering on the Rhine, Alps, and Pyrenees to unite politically, economically, and strategically. Create of this entity the third planetary power and, if necessary, become one day the arbiter between the Anglo-Saxons and the Soviet camp.

The Europe of de Gaulle's dream was partly a way of getting even with the Americans, for whom he had by now developed what Secretary of State Sumner Welles described in 1945 as 'an almost morbid distrust'.

But independence from the United States required a capacity to play off the two great Powers, and de Gaulle was to be bitterly disappointed in the degree of backing he could expect from Moscow. As might have been expected, his first foreign visit, after his triumphal return to Paris, was to Stalin. The ageing Soviet tyrant certainly impressed him: 'In his person and on all subjects I found before me a cunning and implacable champion of a Russia overwhelmed by suffering and tyranny, but a man burning with national ambition.' All the same the visit was a diplomatic fiasco. Despite banquets at the Kremlin and a pact of non-aggression (very similar to the one previously signed by Churchill and Stalin: de Gaulle flatly refused Churchill's suggestion for a tri-partite agreement instead) the Russians refused to give the least support to the French aims: the dismantling of the German state, the creation of an independent Rhineland under French protection, and the internationalization of the Ruhr to provide fuel for Germany's liberated neighbours. When, in the summer of 1945, the Allied leaders met for the last time at Potsdam, the General was not even invited.

All this only confirmed his view that France, to be respected, must be strong. On his return to Paris, he was, as his *Memoirs* show, far more concerned with the hopeless task of trying to re-establish French power in Indo-China and the Middle East than with coping with French domestic recovery. But the General's yearning for military glory evoked no response from the average

Frenchman, still struggling to obtain life's basic necessities. That is why, despite the ecstatic welcome he had received on his return to Paris only eighteen months before, there was no public outcry when, in January 1946, the Socialists moved to cut his military budget. The General, mistakenly convinced that they could not do without him, indignantly resigned.

His retirement lasted twelve years, giving him plenty of time to ponder the nature of power and the type of Europe France could sponsor. He could no longer hope to build French authority on its overseas possessions. If France was to recover great-power status it must be on continental, not imperial, foundations. He would, therefore, depend on German support. Thus he had to adjust himself to thinking of Germany in the singular, instead of as 'the Germanies', and give up his earlier aim of restoring the pre-Bismarckian states and principalities. His purposes, nevertheless, remained constant: a group of nations clustering around himself and France, dominated by France's power and prestige and enabling him, de Gaulle, to speak in their name, as the representative of Europe.

But while the General in retirement was rethinking his Europe and basing it on the traditional concert of nations, far more radical ideas were gaining ground: ideas which challenged the concept of nationalism itself.

For the shattering of the great national states of Europe during the war had opened the way towards a rethinking of the relevance of old frontiers. The nation-state had in too many cases betrayed its citizens for them to identify themselves with its survival. Nationalism, in its Fascist excesses, had so clearly run amok that people were ready to examine new forms of human groupings and other outlets for energy and service. The principal consequence of the revulsion against nationalism was to revive the idea of uniting Europe. This was not, of course, a post-war invention. It had been widely canvassed among the Romantics of the nineteenth century. As early as 1849, under the aegis of Victor Hugo, a Paris congress of the 'Friends of Peace' launched a public appeal for a United States of Europe. The museum devoted to Hugo's memory in the Place des Vosges, Paris's most beautiful square, displays a declaration in large clear handwriting penned by Hugo himself:

41

I represent a Party which does not yet exist, the Party of revolution and civilization.

This Party will make the twentieth century.

From it will emerge the United States of Europe and then the United States of the World.

In the same period the case for breaking down national barriers in the cause of progress was automatically written into the political programmes of all the socialist, revolutionary, and syndicalist groups that proliferated all over Europe. Changes in the techniques of production were increasingly giving the advantage to big business and mass markets; and the technological revolution further increased the pressure towards large-scale enterprises.

On a government level, the case for a single European unit was first put forward in 1931 by the moderate left-wing leader, Aristide Briand, who advocated European federal union in a resolution before the League of Nations. But his own death and Hitler's rise to power shelved the issue until Europe had learnt once more, the hard way, that the combination of old nationalisms and modern technology meant total disaster.

After the war, it soon became apparent that there were wide differences of view on how close the union should be. The choice ranged all the way from federalism to loose inter-governmental arrangements in which each state preserved absolute sovereignty.

Once again it was France, true to her own conception of herself as the seed-bed of political doctrine, which produced the two men who most neatly embodied the two opposite notions of what European unity implies. On the one hand there was de Gaulle, who saw European union as a cluster of nation-states around France. On the other hand there was Jean Monnet, 'Mr Europe', who believed that all nation-states, including France, had had their day, and that modern society should develop a wider, supranational framework.

The contrast between these two antagonists was physical as well as mental. De Gaulle, with his large, sprawling figure, protruding nose, high and sometimes squeaky voice, and his weak and rapidly fading eyesight, had an air of disillusion and dyspepsia. Monnet, the former brandy merchant, small and compact, with chubby hands, a pug-like face, a lively manner, and a warm, pleasant voice, radiated common sense and optimism. The General spoke slowly, cryptically, and ambiguously. Monnet bubbled away at high speed but with extreme precision. The General was confident that he embodied the glory of France and, though he accepted confidence and trust, gave neither. (He once – so the story goes – ended his prayers in his private chapel by rising to his feet and saying '*Seigneur, ayez confiance en moi*'!) Monnet, on the contrary, largely worked by means of well-placed, trusted disciples. Monnet had friends all over the world; the General took pride in having none.

The two men who were to play such key roles in post-war history first met in highly dramatic circumstances. At the time of France's collapse in 1940 Monnet was already stationed in London as chairman of the Franco–British supply mission. De Gaulle appeared first in London on 9 June, barely a week after he had been named Under-Secretary for War in the Reynaud cabinet, and sought Monnet's help in trying unsuccessfully to persuade the British to throw the R.A.F. into the battle for France. Then he went back to France to watch the headlong retreat, and flew to London again on 15 June to try and arrange for the embarkation of the French Government, and as much of the Army as possible, hoping to continue the war from Africa.

Early next morning, while the General was still shaving, Monnet came into his room at the Hyde Park Hotel, with the French Ambassador, M. Corbin, and laid before him the most drastic scheme for supranational integration that anyone has ever presented, on a government level, before or since. Monnet was asking General de Gaulle (of all people) to go and persuade Winston Churchill (of all people) to abolish the French and British nations. The draft he laid before de Gaulle declared dramatically that 'France and Great Britain would no longer be two nations, but a single Franco–British state', with a single war cabinet running a single war effort, and with single citizenship and associated parliaments. (In the excitement the Royal Family itself was forgotten.)

Both de Gaulle and Churchill were at first shocked by Monnet's idea, but at that desperate moment they were both ready to try anything to revive Prime Minister Paul Reynaud's faltering morale.

Invited, with Monnet, to lunch with the Prime Minister at the Carlton Club, de Gaulle took the opportunity of scolding Churchill, for the first but not the last time, for having agreed the day before that the French could sign a separate armistice, on conditions they sailed the French Navy into British ports. De Gaulle urged instead that the French Government must continue the war from North Africa. This was the context in which he pleaded the case for the first – and least successful – of the 'Monnet plans': the plan for Franco–British Union.

Churchill replied he had heard of it already, and was doubtful; but by the end of the meeting he yielded to de Gaulle's assurance that it could still swing the French Cabinet.

After lunch the three men walked over to Downing Street. While Monnet and de Gaulle stayed in an adjoining room, the War Cabinet met. To Churchill's astonishment, the Cabinet approved the declaration almost exactly as drafted by Monnet.

Finally the doors of the Cabinet Room were flung open and Churchill, followed by his ministers, came out to announce agreement. De Gaulle immediately picked up the telephone and called the French Prime Minister at Bordeaux. At the other end, Reynaud could hardly believe his ears; he took out his big golden pencil and asked de Gaulle to dictate him the text word for word. Churchill tells us the General did so with 'unwonted enthusiasm' – the last time he was to show enthusiasm for any Monnet proposal. Still Reynaud remained incredulous and de Gaulle handed the receiver to Churchill, who, speaking in English, reassured him that this was a solemn Cabinet decision.

Staggering under the magnitude of the new commitment, Churchill promptly arranged a three-party delegation – himself, Clement Attlee for the Labour Party, and Sir Archibald Sinclair for the Liberals – plus the Chiefs of Staff and a group of high officials, to leave for a meeting on board H.M.S. *Berkeley* off the Britanny coast, where Britain and France could publicly announce agreement. The British party was to travel to Southampton the same evening. Mrs Churchill came to Waterloo Station to see them off.

But de Gaulle's faith in Reynaud, and Reynaud's faith in his own cabinet, proved excessive. Reynaud later described how the French ministers almost unanimously suspected Great Britain of trying to turn France into a dominion. Faced with overwhelming opposition, he felt he had no alternative but to resign. 'Rarely', Churchill wrote afterwards, 'has such a generous proposition met such a hostile reception.' The news of Reynaud's resignation was rushed to Waterloo just in time to stop the train leaving. Reynaud had fallen, and France, in violation of its pledges, was suing for a separate peace.

The General had never taken the Monnet proposal as more than a tactical move in what later came to be known as psychological warfare. Monnet himself, commenting on it afterwards, said: 'Of course my plan couldn't have saved France from defeat. But it would have provided an inspiration to the world and a wider international framework for our war effort. It might also have aroused America's dormant sympathy.'

With the rejection of the Franco–British union the two Frenchmen were now reaching the parting of the ways, leading them ultimately to become each other's implacable enemies. For de Gaulle, the capitulation was unworthy of his idea of 'the real France', and the government that carried it out forfeited its right to be obeyed. Then his first and most celebrated 'no' was to the legally elected French Government of which, in de Gaulle's view, only he himself, the Under Secretary for National Defence, preserved the right to speak for France.

Two days later on 18 June he was on the air announcing that the struggle would go on and appealing to the French people to support him.

One of those who refused was Jean Monnet, who unavailingly pleaded with senior British officials against setting up a resistance organization under de Gaulle's leadership in England. Monnet still hoped, at that time, that a French Government might be set up in North Africa 'under the authority of leaders installed in office by regular methods, i.e. by a government not functioning under enemy control'. Monnet evidently did not think that de Gaulle's installation was 'regular'. He himself had already decided to work on for Allied victory, but refused to place himself under the General's orders.

Instead, Monnet spent most of the war in Washington working on inter-Allied economic and financial questions. It would never have occurred to him, as it did to de Gaulle, that it was 'neither legal nor moral' to serve a foreign power.

Washington was quick to succumb to the persuasive personality of its irrepressible visitor, and it was in this period that Monnet laid the foundations of influence he was to exercise over American policy for no less than twenty years to come.

His most difficult task was to help the Americans to sort out the North African tangle. He was sent to help the U.S. nominee and de Gaulle's rival General Giraud, and wrote speeches for him, trying to make him democratically acceptable. De Gaulle has certainly not forgotten this episode, although subsequently Monnet contributed to the peaceful transfer of power to the Free French while smoothing over American objections.

Many years later, from the rostrum at Strasbourg, Harold Macmillan, who had been at Eisenhower's North African headquarters, commended Monnet's 'sagacity and patience in that intricate and complex situation'.

Though by the end of the war both de Gaulle and Monnet had firm, and quite opposite, views on how Europe should develop, Stalin was more important than either of them in driving Western Europe to unite. And as the Communists lunged to the Elbe, the most eloquent European in rallying Western Europe against the growing Soviet challenge was not a continental, but Winston Churchill.

In September 1946, a year after he had been rejected by the British electorate but while he was still internationally by far the most respected of all the wartime leaders, Churchill took the occasion of a visit to Zürich to deliver his first public appeal for a United States of Europe. He declared it 'could make Europe, or the greater part of it, as free and as happy as Switzerland', and paid tribute to Aristide Briand and the veteran European federalist, Count Coudenhove Calergi, for promoting it.

'The United States supports this grand design [of the United Nations],' he said. 'We in Britain have our own Commonwealth of Nations. These do not weaken, on the contrary they strengthen the United Nations. Why then should there not be a European group, which could give a sense of enlarged patriotism and common citizenship to the downhearted people of this turbulent and mighty continent, and why should it not take its place with other great powers in shaping the destinies of men? Great Britain, the British Commonwealth, mighty America, and, I trust, Soviet Russia – for then, indeed, all would be well – must be the friends and sponsors of the new Europe.'

For the continentals, however, this was not good enough. Britain, now, is knocking on Europe's door; but seventeen years ago, things were the other way round. Germany's neighbours were still haunted by the 1940 débâcle, and wanted the kind of British commitment to Europe which would insure them against another Dunkirk.

Churchill himself, after a bad start, was quick to appreciate that the unity of Western Europe, and Germany's full admission to it, required more from Britain than applause from the sidelines. Not that Churchill ever really abandoned the idea of Britain's extra-European status as head of a world-wide community and joint leader, with the United States, of the English-speaking world. (He left it to Macmillan to adjust the Conservative Party to the brute fact that the war had left Britain militarily and economically diminished.) But he was ready with characteristic zeal to offer his oratorical talents to the European cause, without bothering too much about the contradiction involved in presenting Britain both as an integral part of the United States of Europe, and, with its Commonwealth, as a separate pillar of world power.

Prodded perhaps by his less empire-minded and more European son-in-law, Mr Duncan Sandys, Churchill personally launched the movement for a United Europe at a rally in the Albert Hall in June 1947. 'What is Europe now?' Churchill asked. 'A rubble heap, a charnel house, a breeding ground for pestilence and hate.' Then he laid before a passionately enthusiastic audience the need for collective European action to help revive the stricken continent.

Less than a year later, at an international congress at The Hague, attended by the whole galaxy of the continent's leading statesmen, left, right, and centre, and excluding only the Communists and the British Labour Party, Churchill publicly preached, to an already converted audience, the case for a United States of Europe. The Congress unanimously demanded political institutions to represent their new-found unity; and from this meeting emerged the

Council of Europe at Strasbourg, designed to give institutional expression to the European idea.

Regular meetings between ministers and delegates from national parliaments were to be held at Strasbourg to coordinate national policies.

But in practice these talking-marathons frustrated their founders' expectations. Before long British Conservatives, responding to the eagerness of their continental colleagues, were joining in demands for a transfer to Strasbourg of 'limited functions but real power'. While Churchill was providing the oratorical fireworks, the humdrum task of organizing committees and drafting resolutions was left to his lieutenants. On 17 August 1949 a amendment was tabled to the Convention that had created the Council of Europe: 'The Committee of Ministers shall be an executive authority with supranational power. The Committee shall have its own permanent secretariat of European officials'. It was signed 'Harold Macmillan'.

A more dramatic move came in the following year. After the outbreak of the Korean War, Churchill himself called on the European Assembly to declare itself in favour of a single European Army 'in which we shall all play a worthy and honourable part'. The motion incorporating this idea was passed at Strasbourg by 89 to 5 with 27 abstentions (including the British Labour Party delegation); it urged the immediate creation of a united European Army under a single command, subordinated to proper democratic control and operating in full cooperation with the United States and Canada. Churchill even agreed to an amendment by his old wartime colleague, Paul Reynaud, that it should operate under the authority of a single European minister for defence. The continentals obviously thought this would be an ideal job for Churchill himself. But Churchill, perhaps with an eye on the next British election, added that he was not himself a candidate. Speaking in the debate, Macmillan said the resolution 'might well be a turning point of history. We have taken our stand irrevocably on this issue'.

In the excitement, European enthusiasts failed to note two important limitations on the Conservative commitment. First, the Conservative delegation in Strasbourg, although led by the grand old man himself, was totally unrepresentative of the grass roots of the Conservative Party. Twelve years later, Lord and Lady Eccles recalled how they, and the small band of faithfuls commuting between London and Strasbourg, were treated in Conservative society as crankish and eccentric. The second limitation was that although the British team were all for a 'European family', they never pretended to share the federal purposes of their continental colleagues. Neither Churchill nor his followers stopped to think how a single army could serve the needs of separate sovereign states. They responded to the Strasbourg spirit principally because the whole idea seemed infinitely remote. But the Europeans thought otherwise.

Here, then, was the beginning of one of the powder trails that was to lead to the explosion of January 1963 and to the exclusion of Britain from Europe.

CHAPTER FIVE

BRITAIN SAYS NO TO EUROPE

WHILE the British Conservatives were thus moving, on somewhat flimsy pretexts, to the top of the class for good Europeans, the British Labour Party, then in power, was establishing itself well at the bottom – a place it was always to retain, though later shared with the Gaullists and de Gaulle.

But, as time was to show, there was no real difference of view between the two parties on Britain's relations with the continent. They seemed divided partly because Labour was in power, and partly because the only Briton capable of responding to the romantic aspect of the European idea also happened to be the Conservative leader. Who else could write: 'I hope to see a Europe where men and women of every country will think as much of being European as of belonging to their native land and wherever they go in this wide domain, will truly feel: Here I am at home'?

These Churchillian periods went down better across the Channel than at home. For the British came out of the war in a xenophobic mood. Probably no British politician, at that time, could have made European partnership a politically alluring issue to his constituents.

Not that the Labour Government tried. From the moment it came into office every ounce of energy and endurance (Bevin, Labour's Foreign Secretary, and Cripps, the Chancellor of the Exchequer, were both casualties of excessive strain) was spent on battling against the series of catastrophes which followed the brutal interruption of Lend Lease in 1945.

It is easy now to look back at a Europe crying out for British leadership and lament lost opportunities. Certainly, the internationally-minded continental socialists were bitterly disappointed to see the Labour Party proving the Ignazio Silone dictum that there is nothing socialists nationalize so well as socialism. The Labour Party's domestic programme indeed could scarcely have

been more insular. Plans were made without the least considera-
tion of their impact on Britain's neighbours. The pound was protected by indiscriminate restrictions, including an almost complete
ban on foreign travel. Naturally, Europeans knew nothing of the
extenuating circumstances. Lord Plowden recollects that one of his
first functions when he joined the Treasury in 1947 was to devise
plans in case foreign reserves ran out. The experts had calculated
that the food ration would then drop to 1,800 calories a day, against
2,700 at the worst moment in the war, and the 2,200 considered the
necessary minimum by the World Health Organization.

Besides, Britain's field for manoeuvre was limited by two over-
riding exigencies of the international situation: the need to
contain Communist expansion which, with the Berlin Blockade
and the Korean War, almost led to world war; and Britain's
military and economic dependence on the United States, the only
country which emerged from the war considerably richer than it
went in. Continental socialists found it difficult to forgive Bevin
for his failure to respond to the trend towards European unity.
Yet any minister in charge of Britain's affairs must have placed
absolute priority on the Atlantic rather than the continental partnership.

Personally, Bevin was less parochial than most of his colleagues,
including his own Prime Minister, Mr Attlee, and Lord Francis
Williams has recalled how, twenty-one years before Bevin entered
the Foreign Office, he returned from the United States convinced
that it had lessons for Europe: 'I do not find any greater genius
for organization in America than here,' he told the Trades Union
Congress when it met at Edinburgh in 1927. 'But what I did find
was this, that I went there from a little island and I was asked to
compare its possibilities with a continent. I found there 130,000,000
people with one economic entity, with no tariffs, with a mobility
among the people to move about without the boundary handicaps
which apply in Europe. I found a frontier 3,000 miles long without
a gun, with commerce passing to and fro pretty freely, and I came
to the conclusion that if we are to deal with the problems of
Europe, we have got to try and teach the people of Europe that
their economic interests, their economic developments, have to
transcend merely national boundaries.' From then on Bevin

obtained a series of majority votes at the Trades Union Congress instructing the General Council: 'To further, through the international organizations, a policy having for its object the creation of a European public opinion in favour of Europe becoming an economic entity.' His ideas were in accordance with the traditional internationalist concepts of the trade union movement. In speech after speech he denounced national frontiers as a 'handicap to us all' and urged the Labour Movement to try and inculcate the spirit of a United States of Europe.

This spirit was the last of Bevin's worries when eighteen years later he took over the Foreign Office. None the less, it was Bevin, not his Conservative critics, who founded the principal institutions which still today link Britain with the continent:

Military: The 1947 Brussels Treaty of Mutual Defence, between Britain, France, and the Benelux trio, was a prelude to the wider North Atlantic Alliances of 1949 and, five years later, to the Western European Union which was the framework for sponsoring and controlling German re-armament.

Economic: The Organization for European Economic Co-operation, first set up to administer the Marshall Plan, twelve years later brought Canada and the United States into the wider economic partnership of the Organization of Economic Co-operation and Development.

Political: In 1949, the Council of Europe, a two-tier meeting place at Strasbourg for ministers and parliamentarians of non-communist Europe, was installed by Bevin, though only under Conservative and continental pressure.

But Bevin took these steps to satisfy not the Europeans but the United States. It was Washington's profound conviction, sustained by Monnet's perpetual persuasion, that nothing good could come out of Europe unless it took its cue from the United States and formed some wider and more perfect union. Disunited, the European states would remain indefinitely dependent on American bounty and, if they did not quarrel among themselves, would sooner or later fall victims to the communist East. The whole 17,000 million dollar Marshall Plan was therefore made conditional on European cooperation.

So Bevin played the European card principally, if not entirely, to satisfy the Americans. But he did not play it very hard. He was ready enough to place British officials at the disposal of organizations for promoting European cooperation, but when it came to the idea of a European authority which might boss national governments, he reacted as uncomprehendingly as Churchill or de Gaulle.

Meanwhile, Monnet himself, the protagonist of a United States of Europe, had taken advantage of de Gaulle's departure to assert himself as director of French economic planning. Monnet at once busied himself with European issues and at first assumed that Britain would naturally participate in any new arrangement.

By the end of the forties Paris was full of young Monnet disciples. They held key jobs in the French planning commission, the ministries, and in the French delegation and European secretariat of the O.E.E.C. Unlike the old-time politicians, who wanted Britain in Europe to balance the Germans, these administrators wanted a strong socialist and democratic partner to fill the ideological vacuum. It was a time when conspicuous wealth, desperate poverty, a rampant black market, and a total absence of any sense of civic responsibility, all seemed to be opening what remained of the continent to a communist takeover. Monnet and his friends made no secret of their desire to encourage British socialists to carry their Fabian message to Europe.

It was in this mood in 1949 that Monnet persuaded his Minister of Finance, Maurice Petsche, to suggest to Sir Stafford Cripps, the Chancellor of the Exchequer, that they should examine proposals for a wider European arrangement. Cripps had always been suspicious of the continentals. At a lunch with Mr Averell Harriman, the principal administrator of Marshall Aid, he had retaliated to Harriman's continuous prodding over Britain's reluctance to 'go into Europe' by asking his American host how he would feel if the United Kingdom asked the United States to get into bed with Brazil. Harriman indicated that he would object. 'Well,' said Sir Stafford, 'that's how we feel about France.'

Nevertheless, Cripps did not slam the door on the Monnet suggestion. Instead he sent three of his brightest economists, Edwin Plowden, Alan Hitchman, and Robert Hall, to talk matters over. It was April, and Monnet characteristically offered them the hospitality, privacy, and comfort of his own villa at Bazoche, outside Paris. The meeting was kept very confidential: it has never yet been reported. For three days Monnet and his colleagues, Étienne Hirsch and Pierre Uri, surveyed the scene with their British guests. The talks foundered in total incomprehension. As one of the participants afterwards recalled, the British were talking in terms of a little extra French beef to add to the British food ration. The French were talking about a supranational edifice to merge the two economies into one. A few months later Cripps sent a private message to Petsche, saying he did not feel the time was ripe for anything beyond the usual commercial treaties.

Monnet was not a man to accept defeat. If Britain was not prepared for the merger of sovereignty which he considered necessary to make union a practical reality, then, as I remember him telling me in 1949, he could find other partners who were.

Monnet is by choice a back-room operator. Now, in carrying out the most successful political coup of his life, and laying the foundations of what was to develop into the European Economic Community, completely changing the attitude of the United States and the United Kingdom towards Europe, and finally altering the world constellation of power, he acted in extreme, almost conspiratorial, secrecy. The American Secretary of State, Dean Acheson, and Ambassador David Bruce were privately informed, and Dr Adenauer and his closest associate, Professor Hallstein, joined in preliminary discussions. But no one in England had the faintest idea of what was going on when the French Foreign Minister, Robert Schuman, on 9 May 1950, suddenly called a press conference in the principal reception room at the Quai d'Orsay, and solemnly announced: 'The French Government proposes to place the whole of the French and German coal and stee¹ output under a common higher authority in an organization open to the participation of the other countries of Europe.' Reading from what everyone knew was a Monnet draft, Schuman announced that the purpose of the merger was to lay the foundations of a much closer union: the ultimate goal was a European federation devoted to the maintenance of peace.

It is useless to examine the kind of Europe which might have emerged if Monnet and his friends had achieved the impossible and coaxed the Labour Government into providing a socialist and democratic leadership for their embryonic union. The new Europe which did emerge was overwhelmingly Catholic and deeply marked by three leaders: Robert Schuman of France, Adenauer of the Federal Republic, and De Gasperi, the Prime Minister of Italy. All three belonged to the pre-First-World-War generation: all spoke German as their first language (Schuman was a Lorrainer, grew up a German citizen and until 1914 practised German law and De Gasperi was from the Tyrol and had been an Austrian citizen and a member of the Austro–Hungarian Parliament); all were practising Catholics with a deep sense of common purpose; all regarded the coal and steel pool as a first step towards full federal union. But none of them shared Monnet's desire to bring Britain in.

Their notion of 'Europe', indeed, even though they championed the same political institutions and used the same supranational vocabulary, was never quite the same as Monnet's – though the outside world, and particularly the British, failed to perceive the difference. Primarily their aim was to create a powerful superstate out of the Catholic countries bordering the Rhine and the Alps: a bastion of Christian civilization against the communist and socialist threat at home and abroad. The Christian Democratic parties, to which all three belonged, were not socially reactionary. But although they favoured welfare measures and a considerable degree of state control they were inclined to lump communism and socialism together as the common atheist enemy. They were unreservedly on the same side as America in the Cold War and saw no objection to American military protection. But their main aim was to create a federal state in which Frenchmen, Italians, and Germans would find a new patriotism.

Monnet, on the other hand, was basically apatriotic. What he sought was an international order wherein the urge of national or supranational groups to dominate other groups would be forgotten. In the April 1963 issue of *The Journal of the Common Market* he has himself described his philosophy:

Unity in Europe does not create a new kind of great power: it is a method for introducing change in Europe and consequently in the world.

People, more often outside the European Community than within, are tempted to see the European Community as a potential nineteenth-century state with all the overtones of power that this implies. But we are not in the nineteenth century, and the Europeans have built up the European Community precisely in order to find a way out of the conflicts to which the nineteenth-century power philosophy gave rise. The natural attitude of a European Community based on the exercise by nations of common responsibilities will be to make these nations also aware of their responsibilities, as a Community, to the world. Indeed, we already see this sense of world responsibility developing as unity in Europe begins to affect Britain, America, and many other areas of the world. European unity is not a blueprint, it is not a theory, it is a process that has already begun, of bringing peoples and nations together, to adapt themselves jointly to changing circumstances.

But to the Christian Democrat leaders, the principal attraction of the European idea was not that it eliminated the power-urge, but that, by locking Western Germany formally into the non-communist block, it would prevent the Germans from using their power-urge to play off the East against the West.

Their solution of 'the German problem' was far from commanding unanimous support. There were always those, even inside Adenauer's own administration, who looked towards the unification of Germany within the context of a peaceful deal with the Russians; they clung to the belief that the Soviet leaders would abandon their grip on Eastern Germany, and accept the humiliation of having the Red flag hauled down, provided only that West Germany detached itself from its Atlantic partners.

Adenauer's critics charged him not only with indifference to the suffering of his enslaved countrymen on the other side, but also with opposing German reunification for reasons of political self-interest, in order to avoid adding large numbers of Protestant voters to the national electorate. But the old Chancellor's real motive was his profound distrust of his compatriots' political stability. He believed the best hope for their future would be to incorporate them into a wider, democratic Western society. Only in such a community, he felt, would they find stability and an outlet for their energies, while becoming accustomed, after the Nazi mass madness, to a civilized life.

It was here that the two separate strands of thinking, the

internationalist and the anti-communist, diverged. The Christian-Democrat 'Carolingians', as their critics called them, were distrustful of any territorial extension of their alliance which might change its political complexion, reduce the Catholic element, and weaken the links which cemented West Germany to the West. The 'Technocrats', Monnet and his friends, saw all national barriers as obstructions to progress. They wanted the new Europe to be closely integrated, so that its advance could not be delayed by the centrifugal forces of national governments, but they also wanted it wide open to others. They believed that as soon as it had proved itself a going concern Britain and other doubting Thomases would press to come in.

Thus, as soon as Schuman had made the announcement about the Coal and Steel Pool, Monnet and his friend, Étienne Hirsch, flew to London to see how Whitehall would react. The two men wanted a straight answer to the question of principle: would Britain allow a European High Authority to take over the control of British as well as continental coal and steel?

While Monnet and Hirsch came to London, one of the key British officials in Paris, Eric Roll, who was destined to play a leading role in Britain's relations with Europe for the next couple of decades, hurried down to Briançon to explain the new project to Sir Stafford Cripps. The Chancellor was convalescing from the latest bout of illness which was to cause his resignation five months later and his death soon afterwards. Despite his distrust of continental connexions, Cripps sensed at once the importance of this new initiative, and returned immediately to London. There he found Bevin and the Foreign Office implacably opposed, and the Labour Government as a whole in a mood to wait and see. But this time the continentals were in a hurry. Within less than a fortnight Monnet had obtained Adenauer's agreement to a draft communiqué. This was sent to Britain, Italy, and the Benelux trio, with an invitation to participate in the subsequent treaty negotiations, but only on condition that they agreed, in advance, to accept the principle of a European authority which could overrule national governments. The continent said yes; but Bevin, for Britain, said no.

Mr Hugh Dalton, the Labour Party spokesman at Strasbourg,

explained later; 'Owing to the initial conditions imposed, the British Government regretfully, very regretfully, felt themselves unable to take part in the talks at this stage. . . . Let those who wish to tread the federal road go ahead and good luck to them!' Even so, not all the Labour Party understood what was happening. In an official pamphlet commenting on the Coal and Steel Pool the Party claimed, quite wrongly, that 'Europeans do not want a supranational authority to impose agreement between them. They need international machinery to carry out agreements which can be reached without compulsion.'

Despite Bevin's no, the British were not entirely absent from the initial phase of the talks on the Pool. Two British officials, Eric Roll from the O.E.E.C. delegation in Paris and William Hayter from the Foreign Office, were assigned to follow proceedings and were given daily briefings on what was going on by the chief French negotiator, Hervé Alphand. But their own personal awareness that something new and important was happening in Europe failed to arouse any response in Whitehall. By this time, in Labour's chaotic last year, with Herbert Morrison succeeding Bevin at the Foreign Office, there was no chance that the case for Europe would be re-examined. It is plain from Lord Morrison's autobiography that the subject never impinged on his mind at all. The only European question that earned a place in his book was a quarrel with Churchill about whether or not public funds should be made available to pay the expenses not only of the delegates to the Strasbourg European Assembly but also of their deputies. Lord Morrison recalls that Churchill shouted back at him 'Keep your — money!'

Since those days, the Conservatives have blamed the Labour Party for its unimaginative response to the Coal and Steel Pool and have themselves taken credit for having been more open-minded. At the time, in May 1950, they did in fact line up a series of speakers in the House of Commons, including Macmillan and a new young member from Bexley, named Edward Heath, then making his maiden speech, to express Conservative dismay. But the fact is that neither side of the House could have accepted a supra-national High Authority. As Macmillan himself said: 'One thing is certain and we may as well face it. Our people are not going to hand to any supranational authority the right to close down our pits or steelworks. We will allow no supranational authority to put large masses of our people out of work in Durham, in the Midlands, in South Wales, or in Scotland.'

Monnet's new community idea seemed wrong to the Conservatives because it relied on technical administrators rather than political leadership. Macmillan told the Strasbourg Assembly: 'Fearing the weakness of democracy, men have often sought safety in technocrats. There is nothing new in this. It is as old as Plato. But frankly the idea is not attractive to the British. We have not overthrown the divine right of kings to fall down before the divine right of experts.'

The Conservatives were also alarmed by the danger that the big continental steel and coal producers would gang up. David Eccles said in the same debate; 'There is a risk that the splendid conception of the French Government will in fact turn out to be a cartel made into an honest woman of colossal proportions . . .'

The Conservatives were able to claim that unlike Labour, however, at least they had a positive alternative. At the Strasbourg Assembly that autumn Macmillan, on their behalf, put forward a plan for joint intergovernmental committees, to concert their production and development plan. The idea was to eliminate the supranational power, which the Europeans wanted to give to a European Executive. The Conservative proposal was criticized by one of the French Catholic leaders, Maurice Schumann (no relation to the author of the plan), as 'tantamount to having the whole Community stricken with paralysis'.

In vain Macmillan pleaded the case for a more pragmatic approach, assuring the continentals that in time of crisis 'we British will certainly be prepared to accept merger of sovereignty in practice if not in principle'. He argued that if only agreement could be reached on an *ad hoc* basis 'Britain might be united in a fit of absence of mind or by a series of improvisations, which would be particularly gratifying to my countrymen.'

Looking back at the record it seems that at that time nobody had a better grasp of the Anglo–Continental misunderstandings than the future Prime Minister of England. On 15 August 1950, at Strasbourg, Macmillan analysed the contrast between the Anglo-Saxon and continental views: 'The difference is temperamental and intellectual,' he said. 'It is based on a long divergence of two states of mind and methods of argumentation. The continental tradition likes to reason *a priori* from the top downwards, from the general principles to the practical application. It is the tradition of St Thomas of Aquinas, of the schoolmen, and of the great continental scholars and thinkers. The Anglo–Saxons like to argue *a posteriori* from the bottom upwards, from practical experience. It is the tradition of Bacon and Newton.'

At the back of his mind, Macmillan remained highly sceptical of the Aquinas approach. I remember meeting him at an Anglo–American press lunch in Paris a few months later and asking what he thought of the Schuman Plan. He told me that he was an old acquaintance of Jean Monnet who was a delightful person but with a foible for constructing enormous constitutional blueprints that had hardly any practical application. He advised me not to take the thing too seriously.

One stray remark in Macmillan's Strasbourg address reads today with a certain irony. After contrasting the British and European attitudes, Macmillan said: 'Of course, the Scottish people, who are the intellectuals of Britain, know that there is nothing to be frightened of: one should accept everything *en principe*, get around the table, and start the talks.' Eleven years later, when this particular Scotsman was shaping British destinies, Monnet suggested that he should accept the Rome Treaty on the Common Market *en principe* and sort out the differences once Britain was inside. But perhaps in deference to his less intellectual English colleagues, or perhaps from political habit, Macmillan preferred the *a posteriori* approach, from the bottom upwards. Had he behaved like his own definition of a Scotsman, Britain would now be inside the Common Market.

CHAPTER SIX

EUROPE IN UNIFORM

FIFTEEN months after sponsoring a motion at Strasbourg that Britain should join a European Army, Winston Churchill became Prime Minister of England. On the continent, there were great expectations that he would end Britain's isolation and take over the leadership of the emergent European Community. As it turned out, in office, Britain's non-European links loomed large, and in foreign affairs the Conservatives broadly took over where Labour left off.

On the European side the Coal and Steel Pool had already laid the basis for Franco–German reconciliation: once German heavy industry was safely integrated into a European system, it had been argued, there could be no revival of dreaded German militarism. And then, quite suddenly, Germany's neighbours found themselves being asked whether – now that Germany was internationally respectable again – it could not safely be re-armed? It was highly paradoxical that for the next few years the drive towards European unity, originally designed to neutralize the German danger, became inextricably entangled with the question of German re-armament.

This was in no way the fault of the Germans who, for financial and political reasons, were still very reluctant to re-arm. What happened was that the outbreak of the Korean War in June 1950 had driven the Americans into one of their recurring panics that the Russians were about to take over the world. Playing their favourite numbers game, they frightened themselves by contrasting Soviet and Western forces along the two sides of the Iron Curtain. They never stopped to think the Russians might be more vulnerable in Eastern Europe than the Americans were in Western Europe: if the Communist conspiracy had at one moment been alarming in Paris and Rome, the nationalist antipathy to Moscow in Berlin, Budapest, Warsaw, and Prague was now a much more dangerous and lasting challenge to the Russians. But by mid 1950, the Americans had convinced themselves the Red Army was poised for aggression and that Germany should be re-armed even though it was only five years after the liberation of Buchenwald and Dachau.

I remember being in Washington that summer and receiving an incredulous cable from my paper asking if it could possibly be true. My own 'sources' at the State Department and the Pentagon said 'yes'. But when I drove out to the north-west surburban mansion off Massachusetts Avenue that pretends to be a château and houses the French Embassy, I found the Ambassador, M. Henri Bonnet, unwilling to believe it. 'No,' he said, 'the American public will never permit it. Haven't you seen this?' And out came the traditional gospel of foreign dignatories in the U.S., the latest column by Walter Lippmann, saying the idea was quite unacceptable.

By the end of September, however, the Americans were presenting Bevin and Robert Schuman, the French Foreign Minister, with an ultimatum: either you let us re-arm the Germans to man the anti-communist ramparts in Central Europe, or we abandon our commitment to defend Europe. At that moment Monnet, usually so sanguine, thought this American move might wreck his fledgeling European community. But the Americans were in no mood to listen even to their favourite Frenchman. Dean Acheson, the U.S. Secretary of State, writhing under charges that his 'softness to communism' had provoked the attack on Korea, was the last man to be willing to wait.

Monnet felt he must come to terms with reality: with his customary zeal, and perhaps a dash of imprudence, he therefore tried to meet the crisis by fitting German re-armament into his projects for European unity. On 24 October 1950 the French Prime Minister, René Pléven, outlined Monnet's newest plan to the French Assembly: France would agree to German re-armament, but only within the framework of a completely integrated European army. Pléven was able to remind the deputies that just a few weeks before the greatest of the war heroes, Winston Churchill himself, had made a similar proposal at Strasbourg. Anti-communist panic, fear of the loss of American protection, and a deep belief that European unity was indeed the route to the future combined to ensure the proposal a favourable response.

By the time Churchill came back to Downing Street, a year later, a treaty setting up a European Defence Community (E.D.C.) under a single European executive, wearing a European uniform, under a European flag, was well on the way to completion.

Labour had rejected the invitation to sponsor the enterprise. The Europeans now waited to see what Churchill, the inventor of the idea, would do.

Five weeks after taking office, two British Cabinet Ministers made totally opposite public pronouncements about the European Army on the same day. On 28 November Sir David Maxwell-Fyfe, the Home Secretary, told the Council of Europe in Strasbourg: 'His Majesty's Government warmly welcomes the initiative of the French Government in forwarding this imaginative plan.' Questioned afterwards at a press conference, the Minister said he did not exclude the possibility of Britain's entry. On the same day, Anthony Eden, the Foreign Secretary, attending a Nato meeting in Rome, formally ruled out any possibility of Britain's joining.

Why the contradiction? What seems to have happened is that leading members of the British Government had discussed the possibility of joining the European Army negotiations before the treaty was finally signed: Eden had agreed to air the idea in Rome. But on his way there he had had a long talk with General Eisenhower, the Supreme Commander at SHAPE, who strongly discouraged him. Eisenhower said that Britain's participation at that stage would throw everything back in the melting-pot. German re-armament would be retarded by, perhaps, several years. The Americans could not wait. Maxwell-Fyfe seems simply not to have been informed that the Foreign Secretary had accepted American advice. Afterwards, the former French Prime Minister, Paul Reynaud, plaintively wrote to the *Listener*: 'The trouble is, I know, that in England statesmen are pro-European when they belong to the Opposition and anti-European when they are in power.'

Churchill might have been more forthcoming had he not run into strong resistance from Eden who, besides being at the Foreign Office, was the officially recognized *dauphin* of the seventy-seven-year-old Prime Minister. On the face of it, it might have been supposed that the old man, who seemed to personify the

British bulldog spirit of independence, and who made a virtue out of refusing to admit other than English pronunciations of foreign words and names, would naturally be repelled by continental entanglements, whereas the exquisitely cosmopolitan Anthony Eden, the devotee of Marcel Proust, and a politician who had first sprung to glory at the League of Nations in Geneva, would be just the man to welcome a new international experiment. Yet Eden had done his best, even in opposition, to restrain the European enthusiasms of his leader. On the very evening Churchill was to deliver his historic speech at The Hague appealing for a United States of Europe, in October 1948, Eden had made a last frantic effort to block it at an extremely quarrelsome dinner party. The row left the two men where they started: Churchill went ahead and raised the rafters of the Dutch conference hall; Eden boycotted the proceedings and went home.

While the Churchill Government stood aside, the Europeans managed to complete their draft for a European Army: it was signed on 27 May 1952. It not only committed the signatories to merging their armed forces but also, under Article 38, to working towards a full federal union.

But for the federalists the link between a European union and German re-armament proved fatal. The curve of zeal for the European Army followed closely the curve of fear of the Soviet Union. By the time Stalin died and the future of Russia seemed wide open, more and more people were beginning to doubt whether Germany's re-armament was really necessary.

As the Conservatives would not sign the treaty, they were asked by French ministers whether they would at least actively associate themselves with the European force, to hold the balance against Germany. Otherwise, they warned, the treaty would be rejected by the French Assembly.

With Foster Dulles at the State Department identifying opposition to the European Army with communism and sin, the British Government dared not openly express its reservations. Eden wrote to Churchill, warning him of the risk of Britain becoming 'the whipping boy for the failure of the E.D.C.'. Cabinet Ministers took every occasion to reassure the Americans and explain that though Britain could not come in they fully supported the idea.

Churchill himself, exasperated by constant American prodding, told the House of Commons on 11 May 1953: 'Finally, we have, or rather we sincerely hope before long to have, the E.D.C., so long delayed but also so intensely needed. This will form an essential component of a progressively developed North Atlantic Organization. . . . Where do we stand? We are not members of the E.D.C., nor do we intend to be merged in a Federal Europe system. We feel we have a special relation to both. This can be expressed by the prepositions "with" but not "of" – we are *with* them, but not *of* them.'

French reluctance to sponsor German re-armament was increased by the de-freezing of East–West relations, which led to the Four-Power Foreign Ministers' Conference in Berlin at the beginning of 1954. Georges Bidault, the goblin-like foreign minister of France, told his British colleagues that in staying outside the E.D.C. they were asking the French to get into bed with a man-eating tiger and then refusing even to stay in the bedroom.

Opposition in France to the European Army came from both Left and Right. The Left denounced the whole idea. The Right, and more particularly de Gaulle and the Gaullists, castigated the E.D.C. as anti-national and accused its supporters of nothing less than high treason. The quarrel shook France with infinitely greater violence and passion than was ever roused later in Britain during the 'great debate' on the Common Market.

It came to a head at a particularly painful moment in French post-war history, when the hopeless attempt to reassert French power in Indo–China finally ended in the catastrophic defeat at Dien Bien Phu. The man who took over the crumbling and divided Republic was a short, stocky French lawyer with a piercingly original mind and quite abnormal pugnacity. Pierre Mendès-France had been the Cassandra of the Left and the bogey of the Right ever since de Gaulle dismissed him from the Ministry of Economics in 1945. Now Mendès-France introduced a new aggressiveness into French diplomacy, compensating France for a long series of humiliations and earning far more popularity and prestige than any of his predecessors or successors, until the return of General de Gaulle. (The General himself said privately many years later that he thought Mendès-France was the only other outstanding French statesman since the war, adding the proviso that 'of course he has no base in the nation'.)

After setting a fixed date by which France demanded and obtained what he judged tolerable peace terms in the Far East, Mendès-France turned his attention to the European crisis. He was not a man to be intimidated by Dulles's sermons, or by his famous threat that if France did not ratify the European Army Treaty the Americans would carry out an 'agonizing reappraisal'. But he did recognize that German re-armament was a condition for keeping America in Europe; and since this concerned Britain as much as France, he saw no reason why Britain should not pay the price.

Mendès-France began by asking his five continental partners to review the whole European Army project to make it more acceptable to the Gaullists in his Cabinet. The principal change would have put into the European Army only the Allied units stationed in Germany, so that the Federal Republic alone would have been left without a national force. Chancellor Adenauer flatly rejected this manifest discrimination and was fully supported by France's other partners.

The all-night session of 23 August 1954 in Brussels, at which the Mendès-France counter-proposals finally floundered, was interrupted by the unscheduled arrival of the American special Ambassador, David Bruce. As he drove up in a very conspicuous American limousine in front of the Belgian Foreign Office where gangs of journalists were waiting for the news, his interference was in all the headlines the next morning and helped Mendès-France in rousing the support of his own compatriots. Saying 'no' to Europe was a ticklish move for any French politician, but saying 'no' to big, bossy America was, as so many European politicians have discovered, a safe way to glory.

Bruce in fact never went into the conference room; he waited in an adjoining library where the Belgian Foreign Minister, Paul-Henri Spaak, now beginning his long career as the most ebullient of the European federalists, and other ministers, slipped out to see him and discuss the deadlock. Spaak's words to Mendès-France that night were reminiscent of those he used almost nine years later to castigate Couve de Murville for rupturing the

Common Market negotiations. Mendès-France replied that he personally did not mind either way, but that it was his duty to report that the French parliament would not vote for a European Army unless his proposals were accepted.

When the conference finally broke up I remember Mendès-France, his face as white as chalk, calling a press conference at 2.30 a.m., while the last edition of my paper waited for the final story. Mendès-France's message was curt. His proposals had been turned down, although he had proved arithmetically to his five partners that the French Assembly would never vote the European Army without them. 'Monsieur le Président,' I asked, 'as your proposals have been rejected, will you personally vote for or against the Defence Community?' 'That, Mademoiselle, is my own affair.'

Next morning Mendès-France flew to Chartwell, Churchill's country home, to tell him that increased British military commitments on the continent would be the French price for support of German re-armament. Churchill replied that he was still in favour of the Defence Community and hoped it would be voted as it stood. Mendès-France returned to Paris, still keeping his secret about whether he was for or against the Treaty, and allowed his Cabinet colleagues to abstain in the final vote.

So, on the last day of August 1954 the French Assembly debated whether or not to discuss the ratification of the European Army Treaty. It was finally killed, then and there, by a preliminary procedural vote. The French deputies, who manage to combine a sentimental reverence for tradition with an extraordinary cynicism about politics, were reduced almost to tears by the croaky and senile voice of their fattest and oldest member, Édouard Herriot, leader of the traditionally anti-militarist Radical Party, as he pleaded for the survival of the glorious French Army.

When it was all over the Churchill Government moved in to salvage the Western alliance and prevent an American 'agonizing reappraisal'. By the end of the year Anthony Eden and Pierre Mendès-France had negotiated an agreement by which Britain agreed to keep four divisions and an appropriate fighter airforce on the continent until the end of the century, and the French waived their objections to German re-armament.

The idea of a supranational European Army, fighting under a single European banner in the same European uniform, was scrapped. Instead a new inter-governmental body, the Western European Union, including Britain and the Six, was set up to coordinate national armies. It had its own permanent secretariat and a consultative assembly of parliamentarians.

Under the new agreement, the Germans themselves undertook not to manufacture nuclear or biological weapons. (Eight years later, a high official of the State Department told me that this pledge had obviously ceased to have any bearing on the new inter-national situation and could therefore 'no longer be regarded as binding'.)

The French Ambassador in London, M. René Massigli, des-cribed the W.E.U. decision as 'a triumph of French diplomacy'. Aneurin Bevan, the Labour left-winger, who opposed German re-armament anyway, denounced the British Government for present-ing it as a British diplomatic success: 'It was a piece of wanton frivolity to bring forward a proposal of this kind and disguise it as a big diplomatic triumph. The Foreign Secretary was squeezed into submission by Mendès-France and Foster Dulles, and, so far from it being a triumph, it was the most ignominious surrender in modern British diplomacy. . . . the European Army could have been ob-tained years ago had Great Britain given the guarantee that was now offered.' In fact, the British Government, harassed by the Americans, would really have been very much relieved, at least in the final months, if the French Assembly had accepted the Euro-pean Army. But to the continentals, Britain's refusal to pay the French price for German re-armament until the chances of a European Army were definitely demolished, looked like just one more incident in the long history of British resistance to European unity.

In any case, with the British guarantee, Mendès-France found no difficulty in getting German re-armament accepted by the Right and Centre parties. The once-dreaded Reichswehr re-emerged as a citizen army which, in subsequent years, turned out to be a lot less alarming to French republicans than their own.

*

By 1957, it occurred to the Conservative Government under Macmillan that as the Germans themselves were now coming forward to provide the first line of continental defence and as the British were badly in need of funds to develop the nuclear deterrent, which that year became the centre-piece of their defence, they could probably withdraw some of their soldiers from the continent. It sounded logical. The British pledges of 1954 carried the proviso that it might have to be modified in the event of balance of payment difficulties; as there were always balance of payment difficulties the Macmillan idea was not in direct violation of the original agreement. But the incident left unhappy memories: no British participant in any of the later European discussions was ever allowed to forget it.

CHAPTER SEVEN

EUROPE SPLITS

DIVIDED, disheartened, and discredited by the failure of the European Army, the advocates of European unity might have abandoned their struggle at this point had it not been for Jean Monnet and his irrepressible team of young optimists in high places. The Monnet network regarded it as their mission to demolish national barriers dividing up Europe, and refused to accept defeat.

The speed and effectiveness of the *relance*, or relaunching, of the European idea astonished the outside world. But once again Whitehall reacted with a mixture of scepticism and scorn. The new European effort was based on the recognition that the time was not yet ripe for a military or political merger: its initiators decided first to attack economic divisions. Once there was a free flow of money, goods, and men, they reasoned, political institutions to manage the new complex would have to follow.

It was from Holland, and particularly from the Dutch Foreign Minister, Jacques Beyen, that the new impetus first came. Early in 1955, Beyen proposed a European customs union, with complete free trade. Few people at the time believed that France, with a couple of hundred years of almost uninterrupted protectionism, could accept the idea. I remember walking round the classically elegant gardens of the Dutch Embassy in Paris, listening to Beyen's radical proposition and expressing amazement that he could imagine that the French manufacturer or peasant could be converted to free trade. In a sense, the Dutch were due for disappointment. Free trade, in so far as this meant not only the abolition of customs barriers but also the free play of competition between Community producers, was reserved for industry only. National barriers were also to be abolished for trade in agricultural products but, instead of allowing free competition in this section, the Six transferred the tasks of maintaining prices and keeping farmers solvent from their own national governments to the central authority of the European executive in Brussels.

At the same time, another new area for joint European action seemed to present itself in the nuclear field. In those days, before the tapping of oil and natural gas in the Sahara, Southern Italy, and Southern France, and before the discovery of vast resources of natural gas in Holland with probable extensions under the North Sea, Western Europe appeared seriously handicapped by lack of fuel. The development of nuclear power appeared an ideal area for European action: demand seemed certain to grow; no vested interest was likely to oppose it; and it required big-scale enterprise which was beyond the scope of most individual members of the Community. Besides, after the bitterness generated over German re-armament, Monnet and his friends were keen to keep clear of charges of militarism. As none of the Six had nuclear weapons this seemed a fine chance to renounce their manufacture and present the world with the first non-nuclear club. (Here again the authors of the project were to be disappointed: Euratom, as the new institution came to be called, was exclusively devoted to peaceful purposes; but France, after considerable hesitation, insisted on retaining the freedom to manufacture her own bomb.)

In practice, both these new plans for Europe were worked out in private and secret exchanges between political leaders of the Six, working closely with the professional 'Europeans'. But for the sake of the general public, the 'relaunching' required appropriate diplomatic trappings and for this purpose a conference was called at Messina, in Sicily, in June 1955. By this time Mendès-France had been succeeded by Edgar Faure, with a more community-minded and accommodating French team.

Once again, the European take-off posed the problem of British membership. A senior French official still remembers telephoning London from the Quai d'Orsay and being told that Messina was really a devilishly awkward place to expect a minister to get to. So once again it was the foreign ministers of the Six alone who plotted the next, and this time commercial, chapter in the story of European unity.

By this time the Conservative Government was less doctrinaire than it had been on the sacrosanct character of imperial preferences. Churchill had publicly declined to be the man who liquidated the British Empire; but it had liquidated itself. The newly independent Commonwealth countries were increasingly disinclined to preserve the old patterns of trade whereby they took in British manufactures and sent out food and raw materials. New Commonwealth tariffs for protecting infant industries were shutting out British exports, and any bilateral deals were seriously circumscribed by the British and Commonwealth commitments to GATT.

The imperial swan song was delivered at the Conservative Party conference of 1954 by Leo Amery. Preferences, he recalled, 'have been described in our official declaration as the lifeline of the Commonwealth which we must preserve. Believe me, it is being frayed away and it may snap at almost any moment under the unfair strain which is put on it.' Amery pointed out that, given the changed currency values, the preferences negotiated at Ottawa now had less than one-third of their original value. He asked the Party to urge the Government at the next GATT conference to insist on trebling them: 'If they fail to act on such a modest suggestion as I have made they will have broken every pledge they have made and gone back on the policies to which they are pledged. This Party has hitherto always claimed to be the material party. Disraeli once said that the Conservative Party is national or is nothing. I say here today that unless the Conservative Party shows by its action as well as by its words that it means to stand for imperial preference, then it will be nothing and deserves to be nothing.' Amery died soon after, and although at the next Conservative conference the whole Party stood up and observed a minute's silence 'in memory of our great Empire statesman' nothing more was ever heard of his idea of trebling imperial preferences.

But the Party's abandonment of the idea that the Commonwealth could solve Britain's commercial needs did not in itself imply conversion to the Common Market. Economically, 1955 produced the first of a series of financial set-backs, but it was only after three more, in 1957, 1959, and 1961, that the Government and public began to feel there must be something fundamentally wrong with Britain's pattern of trade.

1955 was also the year when Anthony Eden at last came into his succession, carrying with him his distrust of European entanglements. He had himself replaced at the Foreign Office by Harold Macmillan.

As we have seen, Macmillan had been one of Churchill's most eager companions in the Strasbourg days. But in office, as one of his colleagues later pointed out, he had not turned out to be 'an evangelical European'. The first post Churchill had given him was the Ministry of Housing, in charge of carrying through the only economic target which the anti-planning Conservatives adopted: to get 300,000 houses built a year. It so absorbed him, his colleagues claimed, that during Cabinet meetings on foreign affairs he was inclined to go plodding ahead through his file of departmental correspondence. His interest in Europe was so inconspicuous that when the *Observer* published a highly eulogistic profile of him in 1958, evidently written by someone who had watched him closely, the word 'Europe' never appeared.

Neither Macmillan nor anyone else in the Eden Government saw any reason to get excited over the *relance* at Messina which neither the British embassies nor most of the British press were inclined to take seriously. The only thing which did impinge on the British consciousness was that the Six were now talking about trade; the Board of Trade, it was felt, should try and find out what was happening.

At Messina, the six foreign ministers set up a special committee of experts to plan the economic *relance*. Meeting later at Brussels under Paul-Henri Spaak's indefatigable chairmanship, the group included some of Europe's most brilliant economists and political tacticians. On the French side there was Robert Marjolin, who had resigned from the Secretary-Generalship of O.E.E.C. to take part in what seemed to him a politically far more promising enterprise. (He was later to be named Vice-President of the Brussels Executive.) There was also the irrepressible, imaginative French economist, Pierre Uri, Monnet's right-hand man, who had played a key role in setting up the Coal and Steel Pool, as well as Félix Gaillard, later the youngest Prime Minister in French history.

The German team included Adenauer's principal confidante, the Permanent Under-Secretary for Foreign Affairs, Professor Walter Hallstein, the future Chairman of the Brussels Executive. Britain sent an official from the Board of Trade, Mr Bretherton, with instructions reminiscent of those given by the famous Cockney mum: 'Go out and see what Tommy is doing and tell him to stop.' The place was alive with excitement, and Mr Bretherton, a tall, tolerant, pipe-smoking Englishman, former economics don at Wadham College, Oxford, with an intelligent grasp of European questions, soon began to feel faintly out of place. The British line was to remind the continentals of their commitments to liberalizing trade inside O.E.E.C. and to warn them of the dangers which might result from dividing Europe. It was essential, Mr Bretherton was told, to make the Europeans understand that if they were again up to their supranational tricks they could not expect Whitehall to take them seriously.

In the practical give-and-take of the committee, Bretherton and John Coulson from the Foreign Office, who came over to help him, participated with suggestions and criticisms. Then, in November, at a plenary meeting presided over by Spaak, Bretherton outlined the reasons for Britain's apprehension, her opposition to any arrangement which might collide with her Commonwealth commitment, and her insistence that the Community must remain inside the O.E.E.C. framework. The continentals listened and at the end of the meeting everybody shook hands and left on friendly terms. There was no drama. Only that happened to be the last time the representative of the Board of Trade or any other British officials were invited to any Brussels meetings. Drawing his own conclusions, Mr Bretherton packed his bags and went home. The Committee thereafter quietly began to draft their report to the ministers, which was to be the basis of the subsequent Rome Treaty, and Britain had nothing more to do with negotiating either the Common Market or Euratom.

At the beginning of 1956, the British Government was still sceptical of the Community's prospects, even though Bretherton personally had been impressed by the high intellectual quality and enthusiasm of the European team. His report perhaps dented London's complacency. For the first time since the Tories had come back to office, there were signs that they were beginning to worry about whether slogans like 'setting the people free' would be enough to keep Britain in business in an increasingly competitive world. The British people were still better off than most Europeans, but Whitehall was beginning to notice a sharp divergence in the rate of economic expansion between Britain and the Six.

What should Britain do next? The question was put to an inter-departmental committee, under Mr R. W. B. (Otto) Clarke of the Treasury, with strict instructions that they shouldn't bother their heads over high politics but simply examine the problems which the nascent Economic Community might create for the British economy. The inquiry was top secret, not numbered even in the normal Cabinet papers. The experts listed a number of alternatives from A to G, presenting different ways in which British and Commonwealth interests could be safeguarded. The most radical project, which even contemplated some degree of supranational management, foresaw a possible deal between Europe and the Commonwealth. Sir Edward Boyle, the young Financial Secretary at the Treasury, found it the most alluring of all, but Macmillan, now Chancellor of the Exchequer, and Mr Thorneycroft, President of the Board of Trade, both opted for Plan G, which the Commit-tee itself recommended. This plan suggested a European industrial free trade area, leaving aside agriculture and consequently most Commonwealth imports. Later, Thorneycroft publicly claimed authorship of the Free Trade project for himself.

In Brussels, meanwhile, Spaak's Report (as it was called, though it was written mainly by Pierre Uri) was submitted to another foreign ministers' conference. The same group of experts were then put back to work at the quaint little castle of the Val Duchesse, a few miles outside Brussels, with instructions not to dare disperse until they had drafted a treaty.

A few days later, the British suggested that all eighteen countries belonging to O.E.E.C. should examine a plan for a free trade area. The Community countries promptly requested a delay so that the new British plan would not interfere with the work at Val Duchesse. Eight months later, on 25 March 1957, in Rome, the historic Treaty setting up the Common Market and Euratom was finally signed.

The new European system established by the Rome Treaty was a good deal less 'supranational' than Whitehall had feared. The Common Market treaty set up a nine-man Commission to run the joint enterprise, but on the key issues directly affecting national economies the final decisions were still left to the Council of Ministers of the six national governments. It is true that the Commission played a major part in their proceedings, as they could only take action on the basis of proposals from this new European executive. It is also true that the Commission could only be dismissed by the Parliamentary Assembly, a gathering of delegates from the six parliaments, meeting intermittently at Strasbourg.

But the six governments reserved the right to name their own commissioners (the big countries had two each) and unlike the High Authority of the Coal and Steel pool, which raised its own sales taxes, the Brussels commission had no autonomous budget and depended entirely on contributions from the national governments. This was a very far cry from a truly federal formula. Even in the preamble, in which the heads of the Six states declared themselves 'determined to establish the foundations of an ever closer union among the European peoples' and 'decided to ensure the economic and social progress of their countries by eliminating the barriers which divide Europe', the word federal was never mentioned.

The clumsy phrase, European Economic Community, and the disheartening post-war flood of initials, which made 'E.E.C.' meaningless to most people, encouraged British newspapers, in so far as they bothered to report what was happening, to use the more folksy term 'Common Market'. But what the Europeans were really engaged in was not just the abolition of tariffs, but the merger of their entire economic systems. This basic fact never really sank into the heads of the British public or its officials.

For the philosophy behind the Rome Treaty was revolutionary. Pierre Uri and his friends, who were mostly socialist, urged that the free play of market forces by the simple abolition of tariffs and quotas was not acceptable in contemporary society. The state, or whatever economic authority held power, was expected to provide welfare, security, and full employment and to increase prosperity for all its citizens. This meant that power over private enterprise and planning of development, previously the responsibility of individual states, could not simply lapse: it must instead be exercised by the wider European Community. This in the long run implied, and was meant to imply, fiscal, social, monetary, and ultimately political union.

Many of the principal sponsors of the new Rome Treaty would have preferred to confine it to the six founder members, at least while it was being run in. Adenauer and the German Christian Democrats in particular would have liked to settle down indefinitely inside their cosy Carolingian frontiers. But there were others, particularly in Germany and Holland, who insisted that the Treaty must be wide open to the rest of Europe. It was on their demand that the preamble to the Treaty included an invitation from the six heads of state to the 'other peoples of Europe who share their ideals to join in their efforts'.

This open invitation worried some of the socialists in the Community; they were afraid that a right-wing majority might bring in Portugal and Spain, thus distorting what they hoped would be a basically democratic and socially progressive partnership.

It was to close the door to these 'undesirables' that Spaak insisted on strict procedures for admitting new members. Article 237 of the Treaty, which later was to be used in connexion with Britain's application for entry, reserved for each of the six governments the right to block the entry of any new member, both at the time of the application and during the negotiations for entry. In January 1963, Spaak and his friends were to protest vehemently against the French veto, but the General's 'no' was strictly in conformity with the clause they had themselves inserted.

Despite the rapid progress of the drafters at the Val Duchesse, who produced a treaty of 248 articles with protocols and appendices in a matter of months, Whitehall refused to be fussed. They contented themselves by observing that the French and Italians had failed to honour their much less drastic pledges to liberate trade and eliminate restrictions in O.E.E.C., and assumed these unrepentant sinners would be no better at redeeming their new promises.

It was indeed true that before agreeing to sign the Rome Treaty the French negotiators had insisted on a monstrously complicated edifice of safeguards and escape clauses to preserve their coddled business community from embarrassment. But what the outside world failed to grasp was that under the appearance of chaos, muddle, and financial irresponsibility the French economy had been transformed and modernized under successive four-year development programmes, to the point where it was already highly competitive. Only a sharp devaluation was needed, two years later, to enable French industry to confound its rivals.

A few months before the Rome Treaty was signed, the Conservative Party Conference was given the official view by Mr Alan Lennox-Boyd: 'Some six European countries are seriously considering a customs union. We can do three things: remain outside, losing rich markets and sources of investment; go in, in which case we would lose our imperial preference system; or we can have some association with it which would give us the best of all worlds.'

The Conservative move towards a free-trade area was warmly applauded in most of the Press. Sir Norman Kipping, of the Federation of British Industries, gave it the businessmen's blessings. But it was hardly the kind of issue which could arouse general enthusiasm. With the national crisis over Suez, neither free trade nor the Common Market was even mentioned at that year's Labour Party conference.

Defending the Free Trade solution meant, of course, rejecting any further thought of joining the Common Market. On 26 November 1956, Macmillan, by now Chancellor of the Exchequer, and on the eve of becoming Prime Minister, explained this decision: 'The countries which together will form a Customs Union will not only abolish tariffs against all goods within the union, but they will also abolish their separate national tariffs against the outside world and will replace them by a single common tariff. If the U.K. were to join such a Customs Union, the U.K. tariff would be swept aside and would be replaced by this single common tariff. Judged only by the most limited U.K. interests, such an arrangement would be wholly disadvantageous. We could not expect the countries of the Commonwealth to continue to give preferential treatment to our exports to them if we had to charge them full duty on their exports to us. Apart from that, our interests and responsibilities are much wider. . . . So this objection, even if there were no other, would be quite fatal to any proposal that the U.K. should seek to take part in a European Common Market by joining a Customs Union.'

Macmillan then outlined the Government's proposal for a wider free-trade area in no way intended to replace or lessen the importance of the Customs Union itself, but in which each member country would preserve its own external tariffs. 'Foodstuffs, whether for man or beast, whether in the raw, manufactured, or processed state' were to be left outside the new agreement.

Meanwhile the Foreign Office was conspicuously looking the other way. The following month, at Strasbourg, the Foreign Secretary, Selwyn Lloyd, reviving the old 'Eden plan', suggested that the parliamentary assembly of the Community should be demoted into a junior branch of the Consultative Strasbourg Assembly. These would also be amalgamated with the Nato parliamentary association, which periodically brought senators, congressmen, and Canadian M.P.s over to Europe for a general chat. Once again, no one took any notice.

So in May 1957, after the Rome Treaty had been ratified, the Paymaster General, Mr Reginald Maudling, was given the task of converting the Europeans to the Free Trade Area. He had no help from the Foreign Office. Selwyn Lloyd felt with some asperity that he had enough on his hands already; and the permanent head of the Foreign Office, Sir Frederick Hoyer Millar, and the Joint Permanent Secretary of the Treasury, a former Foreign Office official, ex-Ambassador to Washington, and old friend of the Prime Minister, Sir Roger Makins, both considered Britain's European links far less important than her relations with the United States and the Commonwealth.

Maudling was a plump, friendly man with an engaging personality, a clear mind, and considerable persuasive powers. His outward show of jolliness and relaxation concealed great strength of character and a hot temper, which he had trouble restraining. In trying to sell the Free Trade Area he made many friends, but his lack of international experience prevented him from grasping what was constructive in the new Community, or from appreciating its importance as a new international experiment. Nor did he appreciate its almost magical political appeal. Instead, he dismissed 'little Europe' and its incarnation, the Brussels Executive, as intrinsically unhelpful and, as far as possible, to be avoided.

Despite the apparent progress of the Six, Maudling did not allow himself to be easily discouraged. The French were of course contrariwise, as they always had been in O.E.E.C., but when the negotiations began, they were a wobbly team. He had been warned that Adenauer would be suspicious of Britain, but he was delighted to find warm sympathy and support from Dr Ludwig Erhard, who seemed far better to represent the true interests of German industry. So for several months this amateur diplomat brashly tried to play off the Germans against the French, and thereby piled up implacable hostility in Bonn, Paris, and, most of all, at the headquarters of the European Community, which depended for its survival on Franco–German friendship.

Maudling was still plodding round Europe when the political constellation changed completely with the Gaullist takeover of May 1958. Many British Conservatives, including Macmillan, by now Prime Minister, welcomed the return of de Gaulle to power. So did Macmillan's distant relation by marriage, Senator John Kennedy. The American liberals thought he was the best man to give Algeria independence, and Kennedy personally had a cult of great men, among whom he included the General. As for the British Conservatives, they could not fail to recall with pleasure the disagreeable things the General had said about the Community and its supranational antics.

But although de Gaulle had castigated E.E.C. during his retirement, it was paradoxically his return to power which saved the infant Community from disaster. French prices had been artificially high, and it was assumed that if France entered the Common Market she would have to invoke all the safeguard clauses to preserve her balance of payments. This would have fatally stunted the Community's growth. But by the general's 17-per-cent devaluation of the franc and a period of subsequent austerity, French industry suddenly became highly competitive. French businessmen were surprised to find how well they fared. After having been exceptionally hostile to the Common Market, they began to compare it favourably with the more bitter competition which would await them within the wider free-trade area.

Opposition to Maudling's Free Trade Area grew. Some of it came from industrialists afraid of competition and some from political leaders who suspected that the wider free trade area would destroy the E.E.C., which they still regarded as an embryonic European union.

But finally it was the General himself who demolished Maudling's plans, not only it seems out of solidarity with his own businessmen, but also as a means of settling accounts with his uncooperative 'Anglo–Saxon' allies.

When the General returned to power, his first aim was to reestablish France's great-power status. In fact during his absence the maligned Fourth Republic had succeeded in getting itself treated as one of the Western Big Three. From the beginning of the Cold War until the Suez crisis regular consultations had taken place on a tripartite level: with the rapidly changing French governments, more French than English politicians had been photographed in the chair next to the American President.

The three were not always, of course, in on each other's secrets. The British and the French were just as much in the dark about Mr Dulles's negotiating plans for Suez as he was about their military intentions. But after Macmillan restored the Anglo-American links, tripartism was dead. Without public apology, he made it clear as quickly as possible that Britain was trying to get back on speaking terms with President Nasser, and the Americans let bygones be bygones. The French, on the other hand, were still at war in North Africa with another part of the Arab world, and American links with Paris were never restored.

The year the General came back, Britain was privately negotiating a new arrangement with the Americans for nuclear research and production. De Gaulle watched suspiciously. In September, he blundered in with a memorandum to President Eisenhower, demanding to share, with Britain, and the United States, a special role in the global direction of Western strategy.

Both British and Americans found the idea embarrassing. There was indeed no obvious reason why Britain should be better treated than France; but there was no reason either why France should be better treated than the Federal Republic. In the old tripartite era, the question hardly arose, but it could no longer be avoided now that the Germans played a bigger role in Nato than France.

The shuffling silences from Washington and Whitehall confirmed the General's worst suspicions. The chance of spanking Britain was right at hand, coming well within the sphere of what the General's business and banking friends told him was good for France. On 14 November 1958, six months after he had returned to power, his purposely provocative Minister of Information, Jacques Soustelle, was given the job of telling the Press that France contemptuously rejected the Maudling free-trade plan.

Two days after the Soustelle statement, at a full meeting of the O.E.E.C. at their luxurious quarters within the tapestried walls of the Château de la Muette, under the presidency of the British Chancellor of the Exchequer, Heathcoat Amory, the British themselves declared the negotiations closed.

For reasons of ministerial seniority, it was not Maudling but Sir David Eccles who was given the job of expressing British indignation. Community circles quite unfairly still regard him as the raging bull in the European china shop. In fact, Eccles had been extremely sceptical about the free-trade plan from the start and was not the least enraged when it collapsed. But a very stiff draft had been prepared for him by the Treasury staff, and although he toned it down it still contained a hint that if France did not cooperate they might later have reason to regret it. De Gaulle's Foreign Minister, Couve de Murville, wrapped himself up in his dignity and walked out of the room before Sir David had finished his speech. He told journalists waiting outside that France was not in the habit of negotiating under duress.

The next morning, in a smaller conference room in the British Embassy, the member states of O.E.E.C. who did not belong to the Community, and who shared Britain's alarm that European trade might now be closing against them, met in secret to plan their strategy. Four O.E.E.C. members – Greece, Turkey, Spain, and Ireland – had already made preliminary moves to set up special relations with the Community.

But, during the negotiations, Britain's special friends, the Scandinavian trio and Switzerland, had banded together to redress the balance against the Six and had got used to combining their strategies. Now they promised each other to stick together and not make a separate peace with the Six. The meeting was entirely spontaneous. On the British side there had been no preliminary discussions with the Foreign Office or the Prime Minister. Yet, as one of the British ministers recalled afterwards: 'We did not exactly prick our fingers and sign our names in blood. But we were in that kind of mood.'

From this little meeting there later emerged the European Free Trade Area, to which the Austrians were invited, and the Portuguese, to everyone's embarrassment, invited themselves. The way was now open towards the much criticized formal pledge of July 1961, saying that neither the U.K. nor any other EFTA member could join the Common Market until all the rest could be 'integrated into a single market at the same time'.

Gleeful headline writers were quick to point out that Europe was truly now at Sixes and Sevens.

CHAPTER EIGHT

UNSPLENDID ISOLATION

AT the beginning of 1959, while the Maudling free-trade area was being quietly swept under the carpet and the seven-power substitute put in its place, the Prime Minister, Mr Macmillan, put on his fur hat and flew to Moscow. Pundits began to assume we must be nearing the next general election.

While the Prime Minister's mind was on higher things, his Government's European policy was 'to build a bridge', to use the officially approved metaphor, between the six-power E.E.C. and the seven-power EFTA. This proposition was keenly applauded by the West German Deputy Chancellor and Economic Minister, Dr Ludwig Erhard, who bought space in German newspapers to feature his own avuncular face and the arithmetical equation $6+7=1$. The West German Chancellor Dr Adenauer, on the other hand, continued to prefer E.E.C. Though he never publicly acknowledged it, everyone knew that, when *he* did Erhard's sum, the answer came to 2.

While Maudling was preparing EFTA, the Six on their side ordered the Brussels Commission to draw up a report on the collapse in Paris. The Commission had always opposed the free-trade project as a deliberate menace to their own single customs union, of which the common external tariff was to serve as cement to hold the new community together. Their report, published while the Prime Minister was still in Moscow, received little attention in Whitehall and none in Fleet Street, even though it was a strikingly outspoken document with major implications for British policy. Whatever Maudling was doing with his end of the projected bridge – and he went on labouring at it for another fifteen months – Brussels was quietly dismantling the bastions on the other side.

The Commission's report was written mainly by an exceptionally brilliant young Frenchman, Jean-François Deniau, then a thirty-two-year-old Inspecteur des Finances – that is, a member of the highest élite in the French Civil Service. Deniau analysed the basic conflict between Maudling's view, that all O.E.E.C. members had a right to equal treatment, and the Community's contention that the Six had special relationships with each other. The Six, said Deniau, 'consider that, having created their Community, having consented to certain efforts and certain sacrifices in its favour, and having agreed to new disciplines and burdens, they have set up among themselves a new association which gives them the right to treat each other differently from the way they treat outsiders.'

Deniau argued that free trade could only be effective in modern industrialized countries if five conditions were observed. First, there must be guarantees that competition will be fair, which means eliminating monopolies and dumping. Second, liberalization must extend to all products and services, including the movement of labour and farm products. Third, economic policies must be coordinated to fend off slumps and preserve full employment. Fourth, regional measures are needed to protect less developed areas which might otherwise be the victims of free competition. Fifth, there must be a common external tariff to equalize production costs inside the countries concerned. In other words, the Commission was flatly condemning both the Maudling Free Trade Plan and EFTA.

Deniau concluded that only two systems could work: either a customs union meeting the five conditions, or else generalized free trade covering the whole free world. In effect, the Commission was saying that those European countries that were not ready to become full members of the European Economic Community must satisfy themselves with freer trade inside the Atlantic Community. The 'Pan-European' solutions for which Maudling was searching were uncompromisingly rejected.

The British Government, none the less, went plodding along as if nothing had happened. In June they produced a White Paper outlining the EFTA plan and explaining the British attitude. At the end of the year they sent Maudling himself into a damp, dismal Stockholm December to sign the EFTA Convention.

In England, this step was mildly popular. The Conservatives welcomed even the smallest allies to redress the balance against the over-mighty Six; and the Labour Party, at least the part of it aware of the outside world, felt better disposed towards the Protestant and mainly Socialist north-western democracies than towards the Catholic right-wingers farther south.

In Washington on the other hand Deniau's report fitted American thinking precisely; and when Maudling returned from Stockholm he received an unexpectedly censorious guest, Mr Douglas Dillon of the U.S. Treasury, visiting Europe on the President's behalf. The Americans, Mr Dillon said, could not lie down and let the Europeans get together and discriminate against them just at the moment when they were making their first acquaintance with Britain's old friend, the balance of payments problem. Like all good Americans, Mr Dillon did not question the right of the Europeans to merge their sovereignties and establish a United States of Europe on the American model. For political reasons, Mr Dillon was personally all in favour of the Community experiment even if it was commercially disadvantageous to his own country. But he certainly could not support a purely commercial arrangement with no political component, which would bring Britain in and leave America out.

From London, where the memories of this disconcerting visit still linger in the Treasury, Dillon went to Paris. There, by formalizing United States entry into O.E.E.C. with Canada joining at the same time, and renaming it the Organization for Economic Cooperation and Development, he laid the foundation of 'the world-wide effort to discover a new economic equilibrium', which M. Deniau's friends had recommended as the appropriate alternative to a European free-trade area.

In May, still interested, the Seven hopefully held a special meeting in Lisbon and declared their readiness to negotiate with the Six. Less than a month later, the Six flatly turned them down. Weeks afterwards, Maudling was still calling vaguely for his 'Pan-European solution', but by this time everyone knew the truth: that the British Government's European policy was in ruins.

In the Community, there was little distress. At the time the Brussels Memorandum had been prepared, most of the nine commissioners who formed the Community's executive would have preferred to keep Britain out. Professor Hallstein, before he became a supranationalist, was the author of the famous Hallstein doctrine, which decreed that any country recognizing East Germany automatically lost diplomatic relations with West Germany. As Dr Adenauer's principal adviser on foreign affairs, he shared, and perhaps encouraged, doubts about Britain's anti-communist reliability.

His Number Two, the eloquent and brilliant Frenchman, Robert Marjolin, had been, when I first met him in 1947, a passionate advocate of founding a new European union round a London–Paris axis. But after years at the centre of the European stage, as Secretary-General of O.E.E.C., he had been disillusioned by successive British rebuffs, and had come round to the view that the presence of Britain would wreck any attempt to create real European unity.

On this side of the Channel, the 1959 General Election brought no outward shift in the Government's anti-Community and, more specifically, anti-Commission attitudes. After the Liberal triumph at the Torrington by-election, the Conservatives had concentrated a special effort on regaining this seat from Mark Bonham-Carter. The Conservative candidate, Mr F. Bennet, attacked him for advocating British entry into the Common Market: 'If there is one subject on which I can claim to speak with some degree of expert knowledge', said Mr Bennet, 'it is about the Common Market, as I have been Parliamentary Private Secretary to the Cabinet Minister responsible for these matters during the last two years.' After listing the dangerous effects of joining, Mr Bennet said: 'This one sentence of the Liberal policy, if implemented, would bring ruin on the British farmer and farming workers throughout the country.'

At the end of 1959, in the House of Commons, Maudling confirmed that the Commonwealth trading system was basic to Britain's relations with the Commonwealth. Signing the Rome Treaty, he added, would involve duties on Commonwealth raw material and the end of Britain's right to make commercial agreements with New Zealand and Australia: 'I can think of no more retrograde step economically or politically,' said the man who was to be Chancellor of the Exchequer less than two years later, while Britain was negotiating for entry. All the same Maudling, a naturally friendly person, did not want to end the year on an unhappy note, and so repeated his belief that the bridge between the Six and Seven could still be built. 'I can say, like Rabbi Ben Ezra,

> '"Grow old along with me,
> The best is yet to be."'

Nothing in the election campaign, and nothing the re-elected Government did or said, could have prepared its followers for the vast unheaval in party policy that was on the way.

As 1960 was rung in, the tired and happy warriors celebrating their third successive victory in a row had no inkling that their leader was to make, before the year was out, what he was later to call 'perhaps the most fateful and forward looking decision in all our peacetime history': the decision that Britain should seek entry into the European Common Market.

How did such a total reversal of party policy take place? To say, as General de Gaulle did in his famous January 1963 press conference, that '*mon ami, Monsieur Harold Macmillan*' had shown himself audaciously ahead of his times and more maturely European than the rest of his compatriots is perhaps excessive.

Already in 1959 there had been the stirrings of new opinion, particularly in Whitehall (the bureaucracy, contrary to its public image, is generally less resistant to new ideas than Westminster politicians). Early in 1960, the strong and energetic Sir Frank Godbould Lee rose to become the Joint Permanent Secretary at the Treasury, and in the course of that year there was a complete change of manpower in the departments concerning themselves with European questions. Sir Frank hesitated a very long time before he finally made up his mind in 1959 that Britain must come to terms with the Community. But once he had overcome his own doubts he was not the man to let administrative tangles or fearful politicians stand in the way. Lee succeeded Sir Roger Makins, a veteran diplomat who had been called in from the Foreign Office to become Economic and Financial Secretary although, as he liked to point out, he was an expert on neither economics nor finance. Sir Roger disliked the Community: his memories of de Gaulle during the war had convinced him that it would be impossible for Britain to come to terms with such a man. Under Makins, the Treasury was thus kept fully committed to free-trade solutions. Under Lee, a new mood was created which gave the Prime Minister himself the confidence required for his drastic political somersaults.

The speed and extent of the change of official opinion on Europe should perhaps partly be attributed to the force of fashion. A young Treasury official, long a convinced advocate of Britain's entry into Europe, recalls that whereas in 1959 the very idea was enough to cause him to be written off as a long-haired eccentric, in 1960 it was getting to be all right and, by 1961, you were a stick-in-the-mud if you thought otherwise.

The Foreign Office too was on the move. The Paris Ambassador, Sir Gladwyn Jebb, who had once shocked a French senator by revealing a strong antipathy for the idea of a continental ganging-up against Britain, came round while still in Paris to the view that the Community was going to succeed and that Britain should come to terms. At the end of his period of office, when he called to say good-bye to de Gaulle, he asked frankly what the General's reaction would be if Britain applied for full membership. The General gave him a long discourse on what a far-fetched and improbable hypothesis that was, indicating that in his opinion Britain would do far better to preserve its splendid imperial preferences and sustain its role in the outside world. Jebb insisted, but what would the French feel supposing we *did* ask to join ? But the General stuck to his view that the prospects were too remote to be worth serious discussion. This was Sir Gladwyn's last posting: after retiring as Lord Gladwyn he became founder and chairman of the Common Market Campaign Committee, the most influential ginger group for bringing Britain in.

The permanent head of the Foreign Office, Sir Frederick Hoyer Miller, former Ambassador to Bonn, always remained sceptical but the new arrivals in the European Department – Sir Evelyn Shuckburgh, back from Paris in 1960, Sir Roderick Barclay, appointed that year to be special adviser on European trade, and Sir Patrick Reilly, ex-Ambassador to Moscow – were all Community-minded. One of these recalls his astonishment when, returning in 1960 from a three-year stint abroad with definitely European ideas, and expecting to find himself in a heretical minority, he discovered on the contrary that all his colleagues agreed with him. In the months before the Prime Minister announced the Government's decision to seek entry, a senior official of the Foreign Office complained that he really hardly knew how to prevent some of his staff 'falling overboard' in their European frenzy.

In contemplating Britain's future relations with Europe, the civil servants were mainly preoccupied with the pound sterling and Anglo–American relations. But the politicians were chiefly worried about the Commonwealth. One distinguished ex-Treasury official today goes as far as to argue that the peaceful transformation of the British Empire into a free Commonwealth of Nations actually damaged British self-interest. It would have been better, he thinks, if Britain had disembarrassed herself of her overseas territories altogether, rather than retain the fake illusion of global power. But, fake or otherwise, the idea of a family of nations if not an Empire, at least a Commonwealth over which the sun never sets, was a comforting thought, in a cold dark world.

Admittedly, the attractions of the Commonwealth for business were declining. Traders who found themselves without warning blocked from Commonwealth markets in the same way, and for the same protectionist reasons, as they were being blocked in other newly-developing countries, were less dogmatic than the Beaverbrook press about Britain's imperial status.

But even with this shift of economic interest, Macmillan might not have risked a showdown over Europe with his Empire-minded rank and file had they themselves not been seriously de-moralized by developments inside the Commonwealth. The first factor reducing Tory devotion to the Commonwealth idea was the transformation of the 'Family of Nations' from a white man's club for ruling natives into a mainly African and Asian grouping of self-governing countries: former dependencies still expected support but were no longer willing to receive guidance, let alone instructions, from their former masters.

The Prime Minister in his 'Wind of Change' speech at Cape Town in February 1960 did his best to convert the old guard to the new Commonwealth. But it is doubtful if most Conservatives measured the extent of the change until a year later, when the enforced withdrawal of South Africa was imposed by the former colonies against the will of the Old Dominions. From then on, for many Tories, the Commonwealth remained an object of hope and charity but was no longer an article of faith.

Other circumstances were imposing on the Conservatives an unhappy reappraisal of Britain's role in the world. Hitherto the doctrine of absolute sovereignty and the idea that it was the duty of every Englishman to be ready to fight for King and Country made it inconceivably shameful that Britain could ever be merged into some supranational group. But in the spring of 1960, the Macmillan Government was compelled to announce the cancellation of the liquid-fuel rocket Blue Streak: this meant nothing less than an enforced British acceptance of dependent status. Britain, in future, would have to rely on American military protection, and abandon for ever the hope of having a home-made and therefore truly independent armoury.

All this produced a new awareness that Britain was smaller than most of its inhabitants had thought. As 1960 drew in, the idea of joining a wider community, which would have been treated as preposterously Bolshevik a few years back, became an accepted topic of conversation at Conservative dinner parties.

Business opinion too was on the move. After a series of financial crises, and with a growing awareness that the expanding markets would be in Europe rather than in the Commonwealth, the business community as well as key administrators began to move in the Community's direction. So did the press. The Conservative papers, the *Financial Times*, the *Sunday Times*, the *Daily Telegraph*, the *Daily Mail*, were backing Britain's entry, or at least negotiations with the Common Market, many months before it became official party policy. The *Economist* had been calling for Britain's entry into E.E.C. since the beginning of 1959, the moment also when it became official Liberal Party policy.

The Labour Party also made capital out of the Government's European mishaps. In the summer of 1960, after the conspicuous collapse of the government policy of throwing a bridge between the Six of E.E.C. and the Seven of EFTA, Mr Wilson, the future Labour Party leader, declared: 'The free-trade area is dead and damned. Europe is looking to Britain for leadership and the Government seems to be in a rut.' But the Labour Party was in a bit of a rut itself. In Europe, socialists by this time believed that their economic and social problems could be handled better in a European rather than in a national framework. Even the German Social Democrats, who had previously feared that a close binding of the Federal Republic to the West would dissuade the Russians from loosening their grip on the Eastern zone, had now changed their minds. It had become obvious, with the total integration of East German industry into the Soviet development plan, that the Russians had no intention of abandoning their satellite. There was, therefore, nothing to be gained by indefinitely holding up development and progress in the non-communist West.

But most British socialists could not conceive of their policies of social welfare, full employment, and economic planning being operated by anything except the nation-state. The gentle and easy-going British Labour leaders would have been shocked to be called 'national socialists'; but they were in truth incapable of imagining the two adjectives apart. Inclined to believe that the British worker was better off than his continental mates, they preferred to reject the accumulating evidence to the contrary. Most Labour leaders and many trade unionists saw the Community (though it was in fact overwhelmingly staffed by socialists and planners) as a neo-liberal jungle. There was very little contact between the British left and Brussels, and the communist smear that the Community was intrinsically anti-socialist was rarely challenged.

It was not only for doctrinaire reasons that the Labour Party disliked the Community. Looking ahead, they anticipated a political merger and, as Dennis Healey told the House of Commons in the summer of 1960: 'I believe that to accept political integration would be inconsistent with our policies in relation to Russia, to Africa, Asia, and the Commonwealth generally. These should still take priority over our policies towards continental Europe.' (In practice, as de Gaulle and Fanfani of Italy later demonstrated, the nations inside the Community still preserved as much freedom as Britain in dealing with the Russians.)

The British Left was also concerned by the charges of neo-colonialism levelled against the Community by the Afro-Asians. Had not three of the member states – France, Belgium, and Holland – in the last few years been involved in direct conflict with former colonies?

In truth, when E.E.C. was first created, one of the principal considerations in the minds of continental democrats was that this new political experiment should divert public passions away from the desire to fly European flags overseas. And they were right. The tricolor could not have been hauled down in so many places so fast had a new Europe not burgeoned simultaneously, giving the French a new sense of purpose.

Nevertheless, the authors of the Rome Treaty were foiled in the hope that the new supranational groupings would have no definite overseas ties. The 'Europeans' wanted it to concentrate on forming a prosperous economic community; this would work out mutually satisfactory trade and aid programmes towards the newly-developing countries, within the wider United Nations or O.E.E.C. framework. Then, suddenly, just before the Treaty was due to be signed, the French leaders of the Fourth Republic imposed a new condition. French industry could not, they said, be opened up to Community competition, if France alone carried the load of supporting and helping its former territories. A special meeting was called at the Hôtel Matignon in Paris, to examine the sharing of the burden. It was long and stormy; the Germans and Italians had other ideas for spending their money, and were extremely reluctant to get tarred with the French and – in some cases where fighting was still in progress – with the Foreign Legion brush.

But the French made it clear that unless they got their way the Rome Treaty would not be signed. Finally a special convention was agreed which would allow territories which had been dependent on the Six to associate with the Community. They would share a joint development fund, enjoy free access to Community markets, and, in some cases, get higher than world prices for their tropical products. But this special treatment was deeply resented by other African states and the idea of being 'associated' with ex-colonial masters was the subject of a violent hate campaign, cheered on by Moscow.

The Brussels Commission did their best to give the recipient countries a share in managing the programme and to emphasize its liberal aspect; but they never succeeded in removing the political stigma.

That was why, during the negotiations with Britain, when the

British delegation finally managed to prevail upon the Six to extend similar privileges to Commonwealth Africans, the newly independent African states, led by Ghana and Nigeria, turned them down. The British negotiators were covered in confusion. But the Labour leaders were confirmed in their view that they had been right to treat the Community as 'a rich men's club', and consequently taboo.

CHAPTER NINE

MACMILLAN SOMERSAULTS

FOR the ageing Prime Minister, the year 1960 was doubly disillusioning: on the home front, after the splendid electoral 'hat trick', an extraordinary autumn budget had to be rushed in to halt the run against the pound. The stop–go policy seemed to be more stop than go, and only accentuated the contrast between Britain's stagnant economy and the continuing boom across the Channel.

Internationally, the Prime Minister had hoped that after his 1959 trip to Moscow, followed by Khrushchev's visit to President Eisenhower, a grand summit meeting could be organized in Paris, for which he could proudly claim paternity. Unfortunately, Mr Macmillan had overestimated the seriousness and duration of the East–West thaw. In Moscow, where I arrived early in 1960, the disillusion that followed the Khrushchev visit to Eisenhower at Camp David was already setting in. The Russians at that time seemed to have deceived themselves into supposing that Khrushchev had successfully softened up the Americans on Berlin. A series of State Department speeches cleared things up. The Soviet leaders thereupon lost interest in a top-level meeting, and furnished with a good excuse by the shooting down of the U-2 espionage plane over Sverdlovok Khrushchev went to Paris to blow up Macmillan's baby. The Prime Minister was badly shaken. Those who have worked most closely with him believe that it was this experience, coupled with the confidential and reassuring advice he was getting from Sir Frank Lee at the Treasury, which launched him on his European course.

Yet to these should perhaps be added a third reason. The Party by this time was itself in search of a policy, and in the course of 1960 the Central Office's thinking apparatus, working out long-term party strategy, had come to believe that a bold bid for Europe could give the party the new look it needed to win another election.

Watching the shifting of 'establishment' opinion, as we described it in the last chapter, one of the key back-room men guiding party policy said privately in the autumn of 1960 that 'going into Europe' was precisely the new challenge the Party needed. He privately predicted then that Labour was insular enough to be relied on to resist any move towards Europe, as they had done before, in the forties.

While the events of 1960 were exposing, as never before, Britain's political and financial incapacity 'to go it alone', certain ministers made their first tentative bid towards what was later to develop into a total reversal of Britain's whole post-war policy. It was Selwyn Lloyd, despite his initial reluctance to get the Foreign Office involved, who finally, yielding to pressure from his own staff, authorized a new and extensive study of Britain's relations with Europe.

From this came his public statement in February 1960 at Strasbourg, regretting that the United Kingdom had not been in the Coal and Steel Pool in the start. Four months later, his junior Minister, Mr Profumo, was allowed to go a little further: Profumo ruminated publicly about whether in view of the manifest difficulties in coming to trading arrangements Britain might not meanwhile join the Coal and Steel Pool and Euratom. The Chairman of the Coal Board, Lord Robens, was by now convinced that the British mines would find invaluable markets among the Six, and the Profumo initiative provoked no serious political or trade union eruptions.

But as the Prime Minister himself came round to the view that something was basically wrong with Britain's international posture and that the party itself was restive, he decided that the Government itself needed an overhaul. The change took place in July, when he shifted Selwyn Lloyd from the Foreign Office to the Treasury, and replaced him by Lord Home seconded by the former Chief Whip, Edward Heath, who was to be given special responsibilities for Europe. At the same time, Mr Duncan Sandys was promoted to Commonwealth Relations, Mr Christopher Soames to Agriculture, and Mr Peter Thorneycroft (who had resigned as Chancellor of the Exchequer when he wanted a 'stop' and the Prime Minister decided on a 'go' policy) came back into office as

Minister for Aviation. Maudling, the hero of EFTA, was moved to the Colonial Office.

Some pundits have assumed that this shift was deliberately engineered as a prelude to Britain's bid to join E.E.C. It is more likely that the Prime Minister's choices were designed primarily to satisfy what he believed to be the pressure inside his own party. Apart from Sandys, whose colours had always been proudly nailed to the European mast, and Thorneycroft, who had become pronounced protagonist during his sojourn on the back benches, there was no reason to suppose that the new team would be better disposed towards the Community than its predecessors.

The key man in the reshuffle was Edward Heath. It was he, as Chief Whip, who had kept the Party together at the time of Suez, managing to stay on speaking terms with everybody during the invasion and the withdrawal. It was Heath, with Lord Salisbury, and Eden, who had made sure that the succession would go to Macmillan.

Heath was the new kind of Conservative: lower-middle rather than upper class, and owing his career to brains rather than to patronage or to family ties. Both Heath and Maudling, rivals for the Party leadership, were intellectually well above the Front Bench average; both were eager, single-minded, and not easily discouraged. Yet as personalities they could hardly have been more different. Maudling was a relaxed family man who took life as it came, and was not ashamed of revealing a certain inclination for idleness; Heath was unmarried and threw all his tremendous energies into his job, amazing his colleagues by his mastery of detail and remaining, in even the most exasperating circumstances, perfectly self-controlled. After Heath had risen to fame, eager research workers discovered that his maiden speech in 1954 had been on an appropriately European theme: against Bevin's summary rejection of the Schuman Plan. But though Heath's Conservative colleagues had known, ever since he was a Junior Whip, that he was setting his sights at the Foreign Office, nobody had any clear ideas what his policies would be. He himself denies that he had made up his mind to seek British entry into E.E.C. until after he was in office and had had time to examine the dossier then being prepared by an inter-ministerial committee under Sir Frank Lee.

Both Heath and Soames seemed to have rallied to the European cause only a few weeks before the Prime Minister's own Christmas conversion.

In his swan-song as Foreign Secretary, July 1960, Selwyn Lloyd laid out Britain's revised views on the European Community. For the first time he set out what were to be Britain's three pre-occupations when the negotiations began: the Commonwealth, EFTA, and domestic agriculture. 'I think it would help if we could be given some indication of the attitude of the Six towards these problems. . . . I repeat we are anxious to discuss these matters. I certainly do not exclude our joining in common interests. In the present state of the world it's obvious that Western Europe must come closer together.' At this point the Foreign Office, who had been working for months on this cautious political re-orientation, agreed with the Treasury that the subject must be allowed to rest. 'Put the files away for a bit,' said Sir Frank Lee, and they agreed.

But contrary to Whitehall's expectation, and thanks to an unexpected prod from across the Rhine, the files did not stay inside the locked steel cabinets for long. Not that Chancellor Adenauer himself was then, or ever became, an adherent of the view that his cherished European Community would be in any way improved by Britain's entry. His friends and his daughters in particular deny that he harbours any anti-British grudge as a result of his unhappy post-war experience. But he has certainly not forgotten that, during the 'non-fraternization' period, he was dismissed from his job as Mayor of Cologne on unsubstantiated charges of having been a Nazi; nor has he forgiven the responsible British Brigadier who aggravated the offence by imposing travel restrictions which prevented him from going to see his wife, dying in hospital a few miles away.

It is in any case true that there were solid political as well as emotional causes for his hostile attitude to the British.

There were two reasons why the Chancellor had favoured European union: first, to resist the communist threat; and second, to anchor the Federal Republic as firmly as possible to the Western world. On both counts Britain, for him, was a doubtful asset. On East–West relations, he suspected the British of promoting 'appeasement' (the Germans never understood how their own use of that word shocked British ears). And, like most continental leaders, he thought Britain would only come into a weak, loosely-grouped European organization that would not be strong enough to provide the necessary anchorage for West Germany.

Yet politics apart, trade figures showed that Germany's economic interests lay overwhelmingly outside the Community. It was primarily in the Commonwealth and EFTA countries that Germany was building up her impressive trading surpluses. For this reason, the big battalions of German business and banking, and their articulate defender, the German Minister for Economic Affairs, Deputy Chancellor Dr Erhard, were constantly pressing the old man to come to terms with the British.

And now in the summer of 1960, the pressure of big business was joined by that of the farmers, who were beginning to object to the Chancellor's pro-French and pro-Community policies.

For the first time the French, supported by Professor Hallstein, Adenauer's own nominee, were insisting that there could be no further progress towards economic integration, unless and until France's partners agreed to extend the Common Market to agriculture. The idea of opening up German markets to French farm products was anathema to the German farmers, who were an essential component of the Chancellor's electoral clientele. It was estimated that over a million German peasants might be turned off the land if French cereals came in at French prices.

The Chancellor was enough of a politician to know that he could not ignore these worries. And so, since he was intending to visit General de Gaulle in July, he felt it would be as well to tranquillize his critics by inviting Mr Macmillan to visit him in August.

Unlike Macmillan and Kennedy, Adenauer had been highly apprehensive about de Gaulle's return to power in 1958. He was afraid that the former leader of the Free French might be an inveterate anti-German, and suspected that he would disrupt the new European Community. His first meetings with him in 1958 and 1959, when he learned of the General's basic dislike of supranationalism, did not reassure him. But by 1960 Adenauer had made up his mind: de Gaulle was accepted.

The General, after all, had restored the order, stability, and a sense of hierarchy, which the Chancellor felt France so badly needed. He had made it abundantly clear that, far from being anti-German, he envisaged a new Europe, based firmly on a Catholic and Franco–German foundation. He turned out to be highly cultured (a quality the Chancellor admired, lacking it himself) with a fluent mastery of the German language and a capacity to quote German philosophers whom the old man had heard of but never read.

In advanced old age (the Chancellor was then eighty-four) a predilection often turns into an obsession. Once he had fallen under the General's spell, and discovered with infinite gratitude that he too believed that France and Germany must be friends, the General could do no wrong. In the many cases where French policies obviously collided with German, Adenauer either found excuses for them, or else argued that other people – sometimes even his own ministers – were to blame. Time and again, he found himself defending de Gaulle against German critics: in French resistance to Nato, in their obstruction to military integration, in the General's public insults to the European Community (which provoked the resignation of his own M.R.P. ministers, Adenauer's political friends in the French Government), and, finally, in the rupture at Brussels. Despite all the rebuffs he stuck to his General.

On 30 July 1960 he and the General met at Rambouillet and laid the foundations for a political framework for their European Community. The General insisted that it should be a loose grouping, a notion totally at variance with the Chancellor's yearnings for a federal United States of Europe strong enough to keep his own and other people's nationalisms in order. The German public was alarmed. To sweeten it, German spokesmen privately whispered that the looser arrangement was better for Britain's prospective entry and hinted that the General and the Chancellor had agreed on the desirability of Britain's admission. This turned out to be false: speaking to one of the few journalists in whom he confides, Dr Fred Luchsinger of the *Neue Züricher Zeitung*, Adenauer allowed him to publish, on 7 August, a rebuttal of these reports; he made it very plain that the consolidation of the Community must come first, before there could be any question of British entry.

When, therefore, Macmillan arrived at Bad Godesberg at the Chancellor's invitation on 10 August, he was not in a hopeful frame of mind. The last Prime Minister to visit Bad Godesberg had been Neville Chamberlain, and though it was pouring with rain there could, of course, be no question of an umbrella. An air-field attendant rushed to get one and held it over the Prime Minister's head during the welcoming speeches, replies, and translations.

Yet despite the disheartening beginning, the visit turned out to be an unexpected, though misleading, success. The Chancellor, mindful of domestic pressure, was extremely anxious to make a good impression. He spoke enthusiastically of Britain's great contribution to the Free World. He showed that he bore no grudge against the Prime Minister for his unavailing efforts to come to terms with Khrushchev. Most important of all, he encouraged his champing economic advisers to suggest a thorough re-examination of Britain's relation to the E.E.C. From this sprang the series of Anglo–German talks which lasted several months, giving the British the illusion that if they did apply to enter E.E.C. they could count on unstinting German support to get them the best possible terms for themselves and the Commonwealth.

Facts proved otherwise: but the conviction that Adenauer had changed his mind and had joined Erhard in promoting Britain's admission was certainly one of the great factors influencing the Prime Minister's decision to seek full membership of the Common Market. But all that Adenauer had really done was to allow his critics a little leeway while he himself went on with his special arrangements with de Gaulle. Two years later, in the summer of 1962, he received a friendly letter from the Prime Minister reminding him of their earlier encounter and expressing the hope that the Germans would help break the already threatening deadlocks in the Brussels negotiations. The reply was curt and unhelpful. The Chancellor pointed out that both their countries had serious agricultural problems and that nothing must be done to weaken the Community. The degree of his indifference to Britain's entry was finally demonstrated when, disregarding all his critics, he insisted on signing the Franco–German treaty one week after the General's 'no' to Britain.

After the fateful Bad Godesberg encounter, both the German and the British governments invited the French to join their bilateral economic talks, but after a moment's indecision the French instead suggested bilateral talks of their own. As in the negotiations with the Germans, the British team was headed by Sir Roderick Barclay of the Foreign Office, a gentle, persuasive British diplomat with a neat moustache and a disarming smile. Opposite him was M. Olivier Wormser – redoubtable dialectician, tall, elegant, crushingly sarcastic, proudly presenting himself as an inveterate Anglophile. His dog-loving went to the length of keeping a poodle under his vast Quai d'Orsay desk. He would explain to his colleagues that he could not bear the idea of Britain losing its fine imperial identity by merging with Europe.

Meanwhile, the British Government was eager not to leave out the other members of the Six. Heath's first journey as Lord Privy Seal was to Rome, and here, as in the Benelux capitals, his hosts keenly advocated Britain's entry. The Italian reception was so warm that the Prime Minister himself accepted an invitation to visit Rome in November, and returned with a blessing from the Pope.

At the Conservative Party Conference at Scarborough that year, delegates were reassured. Heath told them that Europe needed Britain with the Commonwealth as much as she needed Europe: our agricultural system, he added, was far better and more liberal than theirs. Recalling that Selwyn Lloyd had said that Britain must wait to know what the Six would do, Heath announced that the whole situation had changed after the Prime Minister's meeting with Chancellor Adenauer in Bonn. He sounded soothing: 'We have a very modest target. It is to try and find a positive position from which we can move into negotiations. But we are a long way from that.' (Not so very long, as it turned out. By the time the Conference reconvened the next year, Heath was head of the team negotiating Britain's entry into E.E.C.)

Immediately after his visit to Bonn, the Prime Minister decided to make more active use of the Western European Union, set up, as we have seen, in 1954 to sponsor and control German re-armament, and now the only international group which included just the Six and Britain.

The small group of 'European' Conservative back-benchers, who represented the Party at the W.E.U. and Council of Europe parliamentary gatherings – and which included the Prime Minister's own son, Maurice had – over the years, developed friendly *'tu-toi'* relations with many of the continental leaders. The government could use them as go-betweens to survey Britain's European prospects without taking formal initiatives which might have provoked once again politically embarrassing rebuffs.

Among them was Peter Kirk, whose father had been Bishop of Oxford, and who had special links with eminent European protestants. He belonged to a private society sometime known as 'Interprot' (to distinguish it from Interpol – the police network), which met twice a year and included among its members Walter Hallstein, President of E.E.C., Dr Luns, foreign minister of Holland, and Couve de Murville, who comes from a distinguished old Huguenot family.

Kirk is a large, ebullient young man with a baby face, whose enthusiasm for getting Britain 'into Europe' had never waned even in the mid-fifties, when the rest of the Party laughed at him in the House of Commons for urging Britain's entry into the newly emerging Common Market.

For several weeks in the autumn of 1960 the W.E.U. Conservative M.P.s were in private collusion with the Foreign Office discussing the text of a bold resolution flatly recommending Britain's entry into the Common Market. A W.E.U. 'general affairs' Committee (of parliamentarians only) was then arranged and located to coincide with a meeting of the foreign ministers of the Six scheduled in Brussels on 17 November 1960. As soon as the W.E.U. Committee had been prevailed on to adopt unanimously the British draft, a telephone call was put through to the villa of the Val Duchesse, where the ministers were sitting, with a request that the W.E.U. group should be allowed to come and express their views. By the time the discussion had ended it was, and was meant to be, very plain to the six member countries that the British Government was by now very seriously considering Britain's entry.

But the British press and therefore the British public were still in the dark. Working along usual grooves, none of the political or diplomatic correspondents realized that the Prime Minister was secretly contemplating a foreign policy somersault. When Peter Kirk, who had himself been a journalist, called a press conference to announce the Brussels meeting, agency reporters alone attended. Instead of trying to discover whether or not the Conservative group represented the British Government's policy (in fact by this time Kirk was working closely with Heath) they dismissed the whole story as a mere manifestation of Kirk's celebrated enthusiasm for Europe.

Despite all these moves and probings, it seems that the Prime Minister did not finally make up his mind on the European bid until the end of the year. The time for decision seems to have come by Christmas 1960 when he took a few days off alone at Chequers, avoiding the turbulence of colleagues at Whitehall and of grand-children at Birch Grove, and surveyed the dramatic and distressing twelve months which had so bitterly exposed the unsplendidness, at this time and age, of Britain's isolation. It was then that he cast himself in the historic role of the man destined to carry Britain into Europe.

The next thing, of course, was to convert General de Gaulle. At the beginning of 1961, the Prime Minister, having made up his mind on the bid for Europe, took off to see him. It was a bitterly cold January, and it would have seemed convenient to fly to Paris and go straight to the Élysée, where the General lives conveniently next door to the British Embassy. However, it is the new style of great leaders to meet in remote and romantic places to discuss momentous issues. A long drive, accordingly, took the Prime Minister to Rambouillet, where the two elderly men met in a vast reception room with marble pillars, before a monumental hearth. The meeting was a great deal less bitter than the encounter in the same place almost two years later, but both men restricted themselves to vague generalizations about Britain's role in Europe. The General made it clear there could be no revival of any multi-lateral negotiations between the Six and the Seven, but the Prime Minister came back believing that de Gaulle was not necessarily averse to Britain becoming a full member of the E.E.C. itself.

Until the Prime Minister had persuaded his own cabinet colleagues that entry was a good idea, it was obviously impossible to be too frank to foreigners. Kirk was therefore asked to tour the six E.E.C. capitals and in each case he was received by the foreign ministers and explored their reactions to the party's prospective switch to Europe.

Once again, the French were obviously the unknown factor. Was de Gaulle, despite his hospitality to the Prime Minister, really ready to share his leadership of Western Europe with Britain, or could he only conceive of a smaller community in which there would be no challenge to French control?

When the Six foreign ministers had received Peter Kirk and his W.E.U. colleagues at the Val Duchesse in November, Couve had been cautiously non-committal.

But on 1 February 1961, at a private lunch in his honour given by the W.E.U. committee with his fellow-Protestant Peter Kirk as host, Couve was remarkably forthcoming. Of course, he said, nothing must be done to weaken the Commonwealth, and the arrangements for Britain to come into E.E.C. would therefore be long and delicate. How long, his host asked? Perhaps even two or three years, he said. But of one thing he was sure: the organization of Europe was inconceivable without Britain inside. It was an occasion Couve had reason to remember with embarrassment at a later stage.

Very soon afterwards, Heath, who had been immediately informed of the green light from France, made a public statement, suggesting that Britain might after all join the Six behind a common tariff wall. The proposal was, however, presented with two conditions, neither of which had the faintest chance of being accepted by the Six: it would have allowed continuing free access into Britain of goods from both the Commonwealth and EFTA: the common tariff would thus hardly have been more than a polite fiction. The whole initiative was consequently – and as it later appeared correctly – interpreted by the continentals as the first move towards softening up British opinion to the general idea of a European customs union.

On 2 March, less than a fortnight later, Couve de Murville, speaking to the Community in Strasbourg, gave what everybody in London interpreted as a beckoning signal to come in. Ruling out the idea of a free trade area 'which would have killed the germ of political union contained in the European Economic Community', Couve de Murville said: 'This formula today seems abandoned by everybody, and we should be looking for another one. Our partners of the Six and ourselves have always said that the Common Market itself is and will always remain open to any other European country desiring to join. We persist in believing that there is in this, for some countries at least, a valid possibility and doubtless the only really satisfactory solution. We persist also in hoping that certain refusals, even though they may have been repeated, will not be maintained.'

This speech finally decided the British Government on making a bid for full E.E.C. membership. It is true that a few weeks later, winding up the Franco–British trade talks, M. Wormser forwarded a short and shatteringly uncooperative memorandum to his colleague, Sir Roderick Barclay: he said that if Britain really did mean to come in it must not expect to preserve a Commonwealth system, since no country could be in two separate regional groupings. Nor could there be any question of preserving Britain's domestic agricultural arrangements, which were evidently incompatible with the methods being worked out by the Community. This was much rougher than anything the French had said so far. But friendly delegates in Brussels, asked to make inquiries, reassured Whitehall that it was only the French way of taking up a tough bargaining position preparatory to future negotiations.

Macmillan, meanwhile, had had to take soundings from the new Government in Washington. It was not long before he realized that Kennedy's team was just as enthusiastic about Europe, and as susceptible to Monnet's influence, as their predecessors.

The key man for Europe was Under-Secretary George Ball, who was to prove not only the strong man in the State Department, but also one of the most influential men in the President's immediate circle. Ball was a much-travelled American lawyer who had known Monnet for many years. He had been employed as Monnet's legal representative in Washington when Monnet was running the Coal and Steel Pool. On Capitol Hill, Ball's foreign ties were not forgotten, and at a secret joint committee meeting, when he seemed to be stating a pro-European case, an intemperate senator sharply asked him to remember he was now in the pay, not of M. Monnet, but of the United States. Wits in Washington said that when Ball was first shown into his office on the sumptuous seventh floor of the ultra-modern State Department, he was heard murmuring: 'Monnet isn't everything.'

In March, Ball flew over to Europe on a special reconnaissance mission for the President. On 20 March he asked to see Heath, expecting a quiet chat. Instead, he was ushered into a large conference room where all the key men who shaped Britain's European policies were assembled: Sir Frank Lee, Sir Eric Roll, Sir Patrick Reilly, Sir Evelyn Shuckburgh, Sir Roderick Barclay, and many more. They wished to know the American reaction if Britain applied to join the Common Market. Ball replied positively, but returned to Washington wondering whether he was being 'taken for a ride'.

A month later, Macmillan was making his first call on the new President. At a reception on the first evening, he whispered in Ball's ear: 'You know we *are* going to do this thing.' He added that informal negotiations for joining the Common Market were going on, but that formal talks could not begin until the Government could be reasonably sure of success.

In all the Western capitals politicians and journalists were now examining the trends and guessing whether, where, and when the Prime Minister would decide. In April, at a Scandinavian airfield, an American journalist ran into a former Treasury official, Mr Frank Figgures, one of the leading British advocates of the free-trade area (now Secretary-General of EFTA) and asked him what he thought. 'Can you really imagine M. Jean Rey [the Belgian Commissioner in charge of Brussels contacts with foreign countries] making our commercial arrangements for us with New Zealand and Australia?' Mr Figgures replied. The American, whose despatches had been indicating that Britain would probably go in, decided to play it down.

On 29 May, the Prime Minister allowed himself to venture publicly a little further. He conceded there were several difficulties – notably on agriculture, the Commonwealth and EFTA – which hindered Britain from entering the E.E.C., but he added that he believed 'elements for solution exist'. At a Western European Union meeting a few days later, the Conservative backbencher Peter Kirk said he was sure the Government would go on: 'We don't know how or when this will happen, but we hope it happens very soon because the suspense is becoming unbearable.'

It was not just the nerves of politicians and journalists that were affected. Business uncertainty began to show itself in slowing down investments.

But Macmillan was too good a politician to be rushed. Thus there was no historic Cabinet meeting at which the decision was solemnly and formally taken: ministers discovered their leader's intentions gradually, at different times. Cabinet meetings were used for other purposes. Looking back, one of the leaders of the Macmillan team of that time says that far more time was spent in arguing for or against threepence on school lunches than on discussing the shape and purpose of a united Europe. When foreign affairs came up it would be for purely tactical business – to decide who would put forward, defend, or wind up the Government case.

Having made up his mind, the Prime Minister's first task was to convince his own deputy, Mr Butler. Macmillan did not tell his colleagues that his decision was made, but instead invited them to Admiralty House and indulged in suggestive ruminations about what might happen if Britain went in. The radical shift in Conservative policy was not in itself a matter of alarm to Butler, who likes to regard himself as temperamentally a reformer. But like many Labour leaders, with whom he had much in common, Butler was basically a little Englander, unattracted by the European idea. He saw no advantage in abandoning control over the British economy to a foreign body, and he was particularly worried over what would happen to British farmers. Had he not represented an agricultural constituency for thirty-five years? So he told the Prime Minister that it would be impossible for him to support any plan which did not keep a safety net under the farmers, to enable the British Government to fish them out if they got into trouble inside the Community. The Prime Minister assured Butler that he would hope this would be part of any negotiations. But could a national British net be fitted into a common European agricultural policy, whose whole point was that national governments transferred their responsibilities to a central authority? In fact when it came to the point, the Six refused.

(When the time came the Prime Minister characteristically neutralized Butler's potential opposition by putting him in charge of the ministerial committee directing the negotiators. Butler's apprehension may well have held back progress in Brussels, but the appointment made good political sense.)

Macmillan calculated that if there was to be a rebellion (though the Central Office is inclined to think he exaggerated the risk, forgetting Lord Kilmuir's dictum that 'Loyalty is our Party's secret weapon') it would not be under the Butler banner. It was not Butler but Lord Hailsham, the Lord President of the Council, who seemed the likeliest rallying point for any resistance. Hailsham, a Fellow of All Soul's, who managed to combine intellectual gifts with highly developed talents for popular oratory, had played a large part in previous Conservative election victories and could have been a formidable foe.

In each of the two versions of his little book on Conservative philosophy, the first written in 1947, when he was still Mr Quintin Hogg, the second for the 1959 election, the word 'European' appears only once in Lord Hailsham's index. In the first he contrasts the advanced Conservative grasp of the unemployment problem with the faulty ideas 'particularly prevalent among those who have concerned themselves with the problem of employment in America and on the continent of Europe'. In the more recent book, in a single reference to Europe, Hailsham regretted that the impulse towards economic unity 'had in some respects widened rifts between Europeans', but affirmed that 'Conservatives recognize that the purpose of a European unity is not primarily economic. Its purpose is to ensure the continuance of the moral values of Christendom, without which life as we know it would be no life at all.'

Try as he might, the Prime Minister could not prod the Party's philosopher into line: several efforts to harness Hailsham's oratorical talents to the European chariot were dodged. From the apocalypse of pro-European sentiment that overwhelmed the Llandudno Conservative Conference in 1962, his Lordship excused himself: his wife was expecting a baby.

In public debate, the sharpest criticism of the Community had come from Maudling, who had naturally defended his free-trade area plans by stating why Britain's entry into the E.E.C. itself was undesirable. But though Maudling had doubts about whether the negotiations would succeed, he was never militantly opposed to them. He accepted a change of office away from European matters while the Prime Minister carried out his policy reversal; and he was richly rewarded two years later when he was appointed Chancellor of the Exchequer.

At last the day drew near. The Prime Minister had carefully arranged to announce his decision on the last day of July as everyone was leaving London for the August Bank Holiday – the moment least conducive to the organization of conspiracies. The preparatory work on the various ranks of the Party, the Cabinet, the 1922 Committee, the key advisers at the Central Office, was faultless. Few other politicians in British history could have executed such a feat: Macmillan was about to go back on much of what he had said and done in ten years of office, including five years in Downing Street, without losing the smallest Parliamentary Secretary or Junior Whip along the way.

Before the announcement the Prime Minister also had to square Britain's two other sets of associates; the six small European countries who had joined Britain to form EFTA and pledged themselves never to make a separate peace; and the Commonwealth, then fifteen independent states and a huge complex of very dependent ones, whose interests Britain was politically and morally committed to defend.

The EFTA group was convened to a meeting at the end of June and told by Heath that, in view of the impending refusal of the Six to negotiate multilaterally, the British Government had decided it would be better to initiate direct talks, with the understanding that their partners would be free to do likewise. The news was received with relief by the Austrians and Danes, who conducted a large part of their trade with the E.E.C. and were increasingly disturbed by their exclusion from their usual markets. But the Swedes and the Swiss were less sympathetic. They finally agreed only to a compromise which was later seriously to circumscribe Britain's freedom of action: Britain's entry into Europe was made conditional not only on the entry of all the other six 'into an integrated European market', but on the pledge that all Seven must go in at the same time.

Finally it was essential to get acquiescence, or at least a promise not to protest too loud, from the principal Commonwealth countries. For this purpose, on 13 June, Macmillan announced that five ministers would go to the main Commonwealth countries to study their views on Britain's relations with Europe. Duncan Sandys went to New Zealand, Australia and Canada, and had his first public row with the Canadian Prime Minister, Mr Diefenbaker. Peter Thorneycroft, the Minister of Aviation, went to Asia. The Minister of Labour, Mr John Hare, took Africa. Heath made a trip to Cyprus, and the Earl of Perth, Sandy's second-in-command in the Commonwealth Office, went to the West Indies.

The results of these visits were in no way conclusive, although later some Commonwealth leaders complained that they had been led to expect better terms than were in fact negotiated. But the ministerial travellers were, of course, only the final courtesy calls after prolonged discussions. To anyone who knew the terms of the Rome Treaty the limits on the concessions which could be negotiated should have been self-evident. In any case when his pilgrims came home, Macmillan could rest assured: when he made his public bid to Europe, the Commonwealth would not explode.

The secret was well kept. On 14 July, the Government booked time on television and radio for 4 August, and several popular newspapers forecasted news of financial measures to meet the latest crises. In Bad Godesberg, where the Six were holding a summit meeting, diplomats asked Chancellor Adenauer what would happen if Britain sought entry: 'Mr Macmillan will never do so' was his answer.

Thirteen days later Mr Macmillan rose in the House of Commons to put the matter straight. There had been no decision that Britain should join or even apply. The negotiations were only to be about *whether* to negotiate. 'During the past nine weeks', the Prime Minister said, 'we have had informal talks. We have now reached the state where we cannot make further progress without entering into official negotiations. . . . The majority of the House and country will feel they cannot fairly judge whether it is possible for the U.K. to join E.E.C. until they have a clearer picture before them of the conditions. . . .'

The most intemperate of the anti-Common-Marketeers, Mr Anthony Fell, sprang to his feet: 'Is the Prime Minister aware that his quite shocking statement, full of double talk, has had the effect on one of his previous supporters, that he now thinks the Prime Minister a national disaster?' By making his opposition sound caddish, he probably rallied waverers to the Prime Minister's side. The Prime Minister could afford to smile. 'The biggest and most forward-looking decision in our peacetime history', as he called it fourteen months later, had taken place with minimum commotion. The Prime Minister's method of inching backwards into Europe had paid off: both his Government and his party were still together.

Continental advocates of Britain's entry were to argue later that the negotiations would have got off to a better start, and perhaps have been finished in time to avert the General's 'no', if Macmillan had launched his new policy with more vigour. But given the state of British and Commonwealth opinion, and public unprepared-ness for the shock, a more thrustful attitude would certainly have been a grave political risk. In any case, prudence prevailed. To the leader, the gamble seemed big enough already.

CHAPTER TEN

BRUSSELS: FIRST ROUND

THE Prime Minister sent off his letter asking for official negotiations with the Community under Article 237 (for full membership) on 9 August 1961. He was beaten to it by the Irish Prime Minister who had already done so on 31 July, the very day Mr Macmillan was making his announcement to Parliament. The Danes came forward a day after Britain. The Norwegians, less commercially dependent on the Six and, although members of Nato, perhaps more sympathetic to Swedish neutralism, did not make their application until the following May.

All agreed that Britain would pioneer the negotiations for the rest. In return it was assumed that the Community, when enlarged, would go up not to seven but to ten.

The fear that the monster union might sink under its own weight worried many people, especially the Commission's staff whose job it was to turn the Six, which already contained 170 million people, into a going concern. Anxieties tended to grow as negotiations proceeded, and when, a year later, Mr Heath called on Chancellor Adenauer at the holiday resort of Cadenabbia, he found the dangers of the Community's over-expansion were very much on the Chancellor's mind.

Nevertheless, first reactions were unanimously positive. Five of the six governments immediately signified delight; the Brussels Commission issued a statement expressing 'lively satisfaction'; and the General himself said that though one should not under-estimate the complexities, he could only congratulate himself over Britain's application, which was, 'good for Europe and good for the world'.

The next problem was how the Six would negotiate. Paradoxically, for the only time during the fifteen months' negotiations Britain and France wanted the same thing: a seven-power round-table conference. The Commission was hoping to be entrusted with a negotiating mandate on behalf of the Community. M. Spaak was ready to form a special group of negotiators who would have repeated the method employed over the Rome Treaty and who would have been kept noses to the grindstone until agreement was reached. Finally, after protracted argument, the Six agreed on a bastard system, which was neither the governments negotiating individually, nor the Community negotiating as a whole: instead the Six agreed to act 'as far as possible together', with the Commission serving only in an advisory capacity.

For Britain it was as unsatisfactory an arrangement as possible: every time the British negotiators made an offer or a request, the Six had to go off for several hours to hammer out their joint reply. For the French, despite their initial objections, as they were from the start Britain's most recalcitrant opponent, the system was ideal. A less resilient personality than the Lord Privy Seal would have been driven to distraction by the long hours he was to spend pacing in ante-rooms.

While the Six were arranging or disarranging their side of the talks, the British were putting together what Heath rightly described as one of the best-qualified teams of civil servants ever assembled for an international assignment. Heading the experts in London, and a genius at getting things done, was the permanent Economic Secretary to the Treasury, Sir Frank Lee. In deference to de Gaulle's view that basically the negotiation was a matter not for the Community as a whole but for individual governments – and that no government was more important than the French – the Foreign Office made the British Ambassador to Paris, Sir Pierson Dixon, head of the negotiating team.

Sir Pierson, who had been a classical scholar with a double first at Cambridge, was, and with his high-domed forehead looked, one of the most intellectual members of the Foreign Service. He had a donnish and detached manner, and a dread of publicity which had him running like a rabbit when he spied the press. He had come to France only under the Fifth Republic, and thus saw the Community in Gaullist terms: not as an international experiment to be encouraged, but as a continental ganging-up likely to be prejudicial to Britain. He grew increasingly sceptical about the chances of de Gaulle admitting Britain, and in the early autumn of 1962 he sent off a long despatch anticipating the possibility of de Gaulle's veto. The warning found its way into Admiralty House; and came back to the Foreign Office files with a marginal note in the Prime Minister's hand: 'Interesting but not convincing.'

But though Dixon was nominally leader of the British team, the man whose personality dominated it and who was generally assumed by Britain's partners to be its driving force and ideas-man, was Sir Eric Roll – an old campaigner in European affairs since the forties.

Sir Eric, born and brought up in Vienna, an economics graduate from Birmingham and a former professor at Hull, came into public service during the war. A little, short-sighted man, with an infectious smile, he was an excellent linguist and a close personal friend of Robert Marjolin, Deputy President of the Commission. He gave the impression of being as happy on the continent – enjoying the good conversation, the food, and the wine – as he was in his London clubs. The Brussels negotiations were not inter-spersed with parties and banquets and, unlike at the Congress of Vienna, nobody had time to dance. On the other hand, a lot of serious negotiations were done over good meals at one or other of the excellent and discreet little bistros, Comme Chez Soi, Grâce à Dieu, and others, where people who mattered exchanged views, plans, and strategy and elaborated deals.

Looking back afterwards, some of Sir Eric's European col-leagues complained that he pressed his dialectical talents too far. Often, during negotiations, the Six managed to agree on common decisions only by covering up their differences with ambiguities and double talk. Sir Eric, however, would examine the texts, expose the weak points, and suggest clarifications which also brought the text closer to the British viewpoint. People were used to being made to look silly by the French delegation, but the French themselves were the first to complain of such treatment from others.

Nonetheless, and despite an irreverent sense of humour, Sir Eric was better than the more 'establishment' members of his team in understanding what the Europeans were trying to do, and in showing respect for their efforts to create a new kind of union. The fact that Heath emerged from the Brussels talks with a reputation as a more understanding 'European' than Maudling was due more to his reliance on Sir Eric, loaned for the occasion by the Ministry of Agriculture, than to the advice he was getting from the professional diplomats.

The British took the summer months to prepare a general plan of action and on 10 October 1961 Mr Heath presented it to the Six, at the first and last meeting to be held in Paris, before the conference settled for fourteen months on the seventh floor of the Belgian Foreign Ministry. Unlike the announcement in the House of Commons, which had been peppered with 'buts' and 'ifs', Heath urged the Six to recognize that Britain had reached 'a major turning point in its history' and that the 'negotiations will effect profoundly the way of life, the political thought, and even the character of each of our peoples'. Referring to the deteriorating East–West relations, Heath said: 'Europe must unite or perish.' Flashing on the electric grin which was to become one of the memorable features of the subsequent negotiations, he added: 'You may say we have been slow to see the logic of this', but explained that there were historic reasons for it.

All this was heady stuff for the convinced Europeans round the table, and Heath invoked real enthusiasm: 'Magisterial,' said a German diplomat. Nevertheless, when the Six analysed the speech they found themselves unable to accept most of the proposals which Heath had laid before them. In suggesting a vague association of the Commonwealth and EFTA, making 'a wider trading unit', and seeking to prolong the transitional period during which there would be no single market for farm products, Heath seemed to the Europeans to be inching back disappointingly towards Maudling's discredited free-trade plan.

Nevertheless the Lord Privy Seal, hurrying back to address his annual party conference at Brighton a few days later, and spurred on by the initial applause for Britain's 'conversion', felt he could strike an optimistic note. 'You will recall', he told the Party, 'the words of Drake: "Every great adventure must have a beginning but it is the continuing of the same unto the end, until it be thoroughly finished, which yields true glory".'

This was the first Party conference since the building of the Berlin Wall, and the Prime Minister, when it came to his turn to speak, revealed a profound change in his own attitude to the outside world: 'We must now accept the fact that the bleak ideological struggle may last for another generation, perhaps even longer. We cannot retire from this contest, but we cannot wage it alone. It is with this in mind that we have approached the question of Europe and of the Common Market.' The Prime Minister went on to deplore charges that he was seeking an easy way out of Britain's difficulties: foreign competition, he said, might be harsh: 'It is a shower we enter, not a Turkish bath.'

But by now, with daily denunciations by personalities overseas, it was the Commonwealth which worried the Party most. Duncan Sandys attacked the issue head first: 'I am myself half a New Zealander,' he said. 'You will therefore understand me, my friends, when I say I'd rather go right out of public life than have any part in breaking up our Commonwealth. ... With our great Commonwealth connexions we shall, I am sure, be able to make an important contribution to the political and economic policies of Europe, but only if we come in: we shall have no influence if we stay out.'

While the Conservatives were being led to hope that Britain could come into E.E.C. with its 'Commonwealth connexions' unimpaired, the Six were scrutinizing Heath's speech and preparing their collective answer.

The first negotiating session in Brussels opened on 11 November and was described by British officials afterwards as 'tremendously businesslike'. Yet from the very outset the Six made it absolutely clear that after an agreed transitional period they would not allow special preferential trading links between the Community and the Commonwealth. The only exception they conceded was for a group of African and Caribbean countries which, they felt, would qualify as associate members. Other members of the Commonwealth family would be treated as 'third countries' – outsiders on whose behalf, under GATT rules, there could be no discrimination.

For the radical elimination of Commonwealth preferences, neither the country nor the Commonwealth itself was in the least prepared. Only the previous year, in July 1960, Maudling, who had remained a senior member of the Macmillan Cabinet, had told the House of Commons: 'The Commonwealth has always relied on the promises we have given them time and time again that we would maintain the access to our markets of their food-stuffs, drink, and tobacco.... Our signing the Rome Treaty would involve putting the policy of preferences completely on its head and giving preferences to Europeans instead. ... Although the Commonwealth has also been extremely helpful, understanding, and sympathetic to our difficulties, they've always felt they could rely on the undertakings we have given them.'

In putting Britain's case to the Six, Heath had naturally adopted an extreme position; he was demanding that any losses in trade suffered by Commonwealth countries deprived of U.K. preferences must be made up by 'comparable outlets' – that is, by markets of comparable size within the enlarged community.

The British negotiators knew, of course, that this was an optimum position and that during the negotiations concessions would have to be made. As Heath's speech was intended to be the first move in a long series of compromises the British hoped to keep it secret. But as all the missions came to learn, privacy is almost impossible in any diplomatic negotiations that involve many people with contradictory purposes.

In this instance, the strong American mission in Brussels, which had excellent 'European' connexions, had no trouble whatever in acquiring the text. Once it was in Washington it did not take very long for the press to discover that the State Department had it. The *Daily Express* (which by this time had started its daily drip-drip-drip campaign of front-page news items, designed to turn British opinion against Europe),* seized the occasion to complain that a text available to the Americans was still being concealed from the Commonwealth. The Commonwealth missions were thereupon given copies of the speech, and in next to no time the whole draft was available to the Reuter office in Brussels. By the time Heath was on his feet answering questions in the House of Commons on the confidential nature of his speech, every word of it was being hammered over the news tickers in another part of the building.

* The campaign ended on 30 January 1963 with the headline GLORY, GLORY, HALLELUJIAH!

From then on, although sinister rumours about the British selling out to wily foreigners gained wide currency, no serious effort was made to keep the negotiations secret. The Foreign Office had appointed to Brussels a highly competent, hard-working, and, for a man in his business, unusually truthful Press Officer named Clifford Jupp. Mr Jupp, a strong personality with bushy black eyebrows and a sardonic smile, became a favourite figure in Brussels. Each evening he invited reporters to a private room in the faded splendour of the Metropole Hotel where, over cigarettes and a bottle of whisky, they were told what was happening. His comments were, of course, free, but his facts turned out to be so nearly sacred that many European journalists preferred his briefings to those of their own officials.

A good deal of the bewilderment about what was really going on was the consequence not of diplomatic subterfuge but of the complexity of the issues, and the opaque jargon of the negotiators. For instance, at the end of the negotiations there had still been no deal on the lead bullion trade, but a compromise had been suggested by the Brussels Commission. This in the official document, released later, recommended '*décalage* of the second alignment of the preferential duties with the common customs tariffs and abolition of the enlarged Community's tariff protection, after the price level reverted to normal'. How was a hapless journalist to know, if Britain accepted this, whether he should report another retreat or a famous victory?

The bogging down of the negotiations for so many months in this kind of detail was subsequently sharply criticized by some of Britain's continental friends. Monnet, for instance, came to London in person to urge ministers to take the plunge – to accept the Treaty with a few general declarations of intent and then, once inside, make sure that Commonwealth interests were properly looked after. Pierre Uri, who had been responsible for much of the drafting of the Community treaties, told his Brussels friends how he had kept all statisticians, economists, and other experts out of the way, while he was doing so and how he had refused to accept their predictions about the effects of a European economic merger on patterns of trade. He recalled how, when he was helping draft the Coal and Steel Pool, he had assembled leading members of the steel industry from all six countries; how each of them had assured him of the ruinous results competition would have on their own industry; and how he had thrown them into confusion by replying that it was impossible for all six to be damaged by each other's competition and that at least one of them must be wrong. Within the next few years the Community's steel industry doubled its output, and production sharply increased in every one of the six countries. Here, said M. Uri, was a warning against undue apprehensiveness.

But the fact was that no British Government would have dared ride a European horse roughshod over a kicking and screaming Commonwealth. As soon as it became obvious that the Six would not accept indefinite trading links with the Commonwealth, there was no other way than to tackle the trading issues on a commodity-by-commodity basis.

The first six months of the Brussels negotiations were therefore entirely taken up by extensive surveys, studies of what items would be effected by how much, classification of Commonwealth trade into manageable components, and examinations of how the damage could best be limited in each individual case. Buzzing round the European missions were the European business and farming lobbies, each with their own hard-luck stories, but, unlike their political leaders, refusing to admit responsibility of any sort towards the outside world.

The results were some quaint-looking compromises: zero duty for tea, cricket bats, and polo sticks, but only a suspension of duties for desiccated coconut and no more than a slowing-down of the introduction of a common tariff for pepper. A special formula was invented for extract of mimosa: the 10-per-cent duty would be temporarily suspended, until after the next round of tariff reductions at GATT, anticipated under the term of the Kennedy Trade Expansion Act. Two days after the General's No, Heath was still in the conference room arguing for Canada's canned salmon, Australia's tinned peaches, pears, and apricots, and for the sultanas of Cyprus.

Everyone knew that the real struggle would come over British and Commonwealth farmers who shared out the British market, though on very different terms. 'The two-tier system' gave water-tight protection to domestic producers but took food from the Commonwealth at the lowest world price. This system was manifestly incompatible with joining a single protected European market. The 'world prices' at which Britain bought were generally heavily susidized by the exporting Governments, and it has been calculated that the exporters were contributing an average of a thousand million dollars a year to Britain's upkeep.

The French deliberately held up negotiations on this all-important topic until they had extracted an agreement from the Six on the Community's common agricultural system. It is highly doubtful in fact whether, in the two hundred hours' marathon meeting which ended on 14 January 1963, they could have achieved terms so advantageous to their own farmers and tax-payers had they not warned the other five that this was a pre-condition of continuing talks with Britain. This argument more than any other seems to have overcome the resistance of the Germans, who kept their own food prices abnormally high to protect their backward peasant farmers and were consequently less keen than the rest in extending the Common Market to agriculture.

Even after this deal, Couve de Murville demanded another five weeks to complete, translate, and distribute the next texts, and it was not until 22 February that the British were invited to make their own agricultural proposals. Heath repeated the case for 'comparable outlets'. Soames joined him, and urged a prolonged transitional period during which the British Government would preserve her right to take national action to protect her farmers' incomes.

The British were by this time reconnoitring the positions of the Six and the chances of a big package deal to be agreed by the summer recess. This 'outline agreement' would give the Commonwealth and the U.K. sufficient knowledge of the terms to decide whether Britain should go in; then, after the Commonwealth conference and the party conferences in the autumn, work could begin on the drafting of the treaty and the passage of the appropriate legislation. This could be ratified and ready for the next general election.

At this stage, in the spring of 1962, Britain offered no concessions: it was thought more prudent to hold them in reserve. This may have been the key blunder of the negotiations. Members of the Brussels Commission, as well as M. Bernard Clappier, the head of the French negotiating team, believe that if Britain had come forward with her essential compromises a few weeks earlier, instead of bundling them in just as the whole Community was folding up for its sacrosanct August holidays, then the negotiations would have ended not in failure but in success.

According to this argument, there would have been no French veto. The General had told his familiars, after his long meeting with the Prime Minister at the Château de Champs in June that year, that he was resigned to the inevitability of Britain's entry. '*Les choses étant ce qu'elles sont*', as the General says, Britain, by now, would be in.

The first substansive agreement between Britain and the Six was reached on 29 May, when they agreed to a little-by-little elimination of U.K. preferences for manufactured produces from the old dominions.

It was perfectly plain that Britain could not enter the Common Market without having the same external tariffs as its partners; it was in order to prevent any sudden ruptures in trading patterns that the Six agreed to slow down the rate of lowering these tariffs. None the less, within forty-eight hours Mr Menzies, the Prime Minister of Australia, and Mr John Marshall, the Deputy Premier of New Zealand, had issued a joint statement expressing indignant fury and warning against making this a precedent for dealing with the much more important agricultural exports.

Already, in Brussels, Commonwealth voices were making themselves heard. Most overseas representatives contented themselves with tabling memoranda, but Dr W. A. Westermann, the tall, gruff, and assertive Secretary of the Australian Department of Trade, insisted on being heard personally at the conference table. Westermann, who presented himself as a simple-minded backwoodsman, showed himself a formidable debater with a perfect mastery of his subject. He produced a considerable commotion.

The French and the Commission watched with alarm the perturbation among the five. Both argued that the Australians' demand for guaranteed markets inside the Community, to make up for the losses of U.K. preference, was incompatible with both the spirit of the Rome Treaty and the letter of the January 1962 agricultural system. Dr Westermann was bowed out empty-handed.

Looking back over the relationships between the Commission and France during the negotiations with Britain, a young German official suggested the analogy of the Pope and the Emperor: the Commission was the Pope, doctrinally defending the Treaty of Rome, and France was the Emperor, wielding temporal power against transgressors. When the two stuck together they were indomitable; when they fell apart, the Community itself collapsed.

As it turned out, the Pope and the Emperor were better disposed towards the newly developing areas of the Commonwealth than towards the old white dominions. The Six agreed, on French initiative, to negotiate a comprehensive trade agreement with the three Asian Commonwealth countries, India, Pakistan, Ceylon. In this they pledged themselves in advance, in terms which have no precedent in the history of commercial negotiations, to see that these countries maintained, and as far as possible developed, their earnings of foreign capital to enable them to finance their development plans. The Six were already providing India with considerably more investment funds, than Britain; and they had a direct commercial as well as political interest in preserving India's solvency.

The agreement was welcomed in London. But New Delhi complained bitterly that it was insufficiently specific, begging in vain that preferential access to Common Market markets should be preserved at least until the new trade agreements were signed.

To Commonwealth countries in Africa and the Caribbean, the Six next conceded the same terms they had given their own former dependencies. This met Heath's original warning that Common-wealth tropical territories 'would certainly not understand if, as a result of Britain becoming a part of the Community, we were obliged to discriminate against them in favour of other non-European countries'. Here was a success for Britain. So far, so good.

The first serious diplomatic infighting took place over Britain's own farmers. An all-night session was needed to fight out a compromise whereby the Six accepted the British system of an annual review of farm prices and incomes, but the British in return gave up the hope, so dear to Mr Butler, of preserving a national net to catch the farmers if they fell. The plan, officially accepted by Heath at 3.15 on the morning of 31 July, provided there should be Community annual reviews based on government reports; if these showed that farmers in certain 'areas' were not preserving their standards of living, the Commission would be bound to help them.

One of the main reasons this argument took so long was semantic: the French, and the Commission, wanted the word 'region' applied to places where the farmers were in trouble, which suggested a particular geographical district, whereas the British stuck to 'area', by which they meant a whole country. This dispute practically broke up the conference before the French, contrary to their usual habit, without any preliminary joint agreement with the Six, suddenly gave in.

After this ordeal Brussels wrongly supposed that thenceforward British domestic agriculture would no longer be a problem. But both sides discovered the following October that there was a still more serious collision of views ahead, on how to handle the transitional period during which British subsidies and prices would have to be adjusted to those in the Community. It was British agriculture, not the Commonwealth problem, which bogged the conference down from October to January and gave the General his opportunity for alleging that the negotiations were going round in circles and should be stopped.

On the Commonwealth, Britain was prepared to compromise. She abandoned Mr Heath's demands for guaranteed 'comparable outlets' and agreed instead to discuss the 'Colombo Plan' for world commodity agreements. This plan was called after the young and soft-spoken Italian Minister for Foreign Trade.

Signor Colombo's great talent was for unravelling knots and unruffling tempers. At the worst meetings, one delegate explained, his voice had the soothing effect of a violin played by a master. Colombo indeed was a highly musical man – a talent which specially endeared him to Mr Heath, who played the organ for him when he visited England in November.

That particular trip, however, was a great disappointment to the Italian minister: it coincided with a very unfriendly paragraph about him in the *Economist* which seemed, though it was not, officially inspired. It complained that he was failing to support the British against the French. This was in fact unfair, as his principal usefulness to the British was his capacity for carrying along the French and the Commission better than Britain's more militant friends, the Dutch or the divided and distracted Germans.

The Colombo Plan admitted that Commonwealth producers (except New Zealand, for whom something special would have to be done) must be treated like any other foreign exporters; but in return the Six would pledge themselves to adopt liberal trade policies, to restrict domestic production by fixing 'reasonable prices', to make sure there would still be room for exports from the outside world, and to start, immediately, negotiations for world-wide commodity agreements that would look after the interests of the main exporting countries, especially the Commonwealth.

The Plan foresaw world-wide agreements covering not only cereals and sugar but also perishable goods, meat and dairy products. The British were inclined to treat the offer as pie in the sky. The Six refused to promise that, in case the pie failed to materialize, Commonwealth preference should be preserved. The most they would concede, if all else failed, was consultation.

The trouble was that neither the French nor the British had the least confidence in the honourableness of each other's intentions. It would be wrong to suppose that the French delegation in Brussels was already working under de Gaulle's order to keep Britain out. They were given the widest freedom in deciding policies. The General's purpose at this stage was simply to make sure that if Britain came in, as he was assuming it would, then France should exact the best possible terms.

Recalling the private meetings held by the French delegation at that time, one of the key members said not long ago that there was not the least doubt that the delegation's main aim then was to secure the best possible terms for French agriculture; whether or not Britain came in was secondary.

The preoccupation was understandable. French agriculture had gone through a rather belated technological revolution and, as the country was extremely fertile, the problem of disposing of its surpluses had become acute. The British maintained that the French wanted to monopolize the entire Common Market for their own farmers, and were trying ultimately to impose a policy on the Community that would exclude the Commonwealth altogether. Heath flatly warned the Six that unless they were ready to promise to restrain their own producers, so as to go on letting the Commonwealth sell in the enlarged Community markets, then there was not the faintest hope that Britain would come in. At the end of July, after four days of intense argument about what kind of reassurance Britain required, a last, long meeting led nowhere. Delegates recall the all-night session of 28–29 July as a long nightmare, with the Lord Privy Seal monotonously repeating the words 'Access, access, access', like a litany.

The main objector was the tall, muscular Dr Sicco Mansholt, Director of the Commission's Agricultural Department, himself a farmer and formerly Dutch Minister of Agriculture, who took all-night sittings in his stride. He protested vehemently that the Community never had any intention of becoming self-sufficient, and could not do so under the terms of the Rome Treaty, which compelled signatories to work for the 'harmonious development of world trade'. The British remained unmoved.

While Mansholt was defending the Rome Treaty the French negotiators were canvassing their own 'Baumgartner Plan' for dealing with the international trade in foodstuffs.

The Plan provided for a general rise in the world prices of basic foodstuffs for the benefit of the producer nations. The French proposed to compensate the poorer countries for a rise in food prices by setting up an international fund to buy and distribute surpluses as aid to the underfed one-third of the world. It sounded wise and progressive – except that the high commodity prices would obviously be more advantageous to exporting than to importing countries. 'People talk about perfidious Albion,' a U.K. delegate said, 'but the way the French promote their national interests under a humanitarian garb makes us look like babies.'

So Saturday came with no agreement on agriculture. The French were unperturbed, but the rest of the Six suspected (rightly) that this might be the last chance: if the momentum of the nego-tiations was broken, how could it ever be revived? The last, full, seven-power meeting ended on the Saturday, and at once, in secret, France's five partners began to meet to see if anything could be done to bring Britain and France closer together. Slowly they worked out twelve amendments to the Commission's 'Paper on Temperate Agricultural Products from the Commonwealth Countries', which had been painfully put together in intentionally flabby prose as the highest common denominator on which the Six agreed, and which served as a basic document for the July discussions.

Wednesday morning, when the Six were meeting together to prepare their joint negotiating position, the Belgians, to avoid giving the French the impression that her colleagues were ganging up, presented the amendments as proposals from their own delegation.

The French, however, knew what had been happening; and M. Wormser inexorably analysed and rejected every one of the so-called Belgian amendments. Towards the end of the meeting news of French destructiveness reached M. Spaak and he came down furiously to the seventh floor (his own office was on the eighth) to complain that the whole proceedings were 'puerile'. He scolded the French for the short-sighted folly of allowing the future of Europe and the Western world to be compromised by arguments about the price of food. Here he slipped up, for, as all the people involved in the negotiations already knew, prices in Germany were much higher than in France. '*M. le Ministre*,' M. Wormser replied, 'surely you should be addressing your comment not to me but to my German colleague?'

When all the amendments had been rejected and the document restored to where it had been left on the previous Saturday, the British delegation were readmitted and Heath recalled the reasons for the British objections.

After Heath had spoken, Professor Hallstein, for the Com-mission, suggested that things were getting repetitive and that it would be better if the British themselves put forward their own amendments. After some hesitation, the U.K. delegation agreed to produce a written document, and the conference was suspended for twenty-four hours while they went to work. Besides a great many clarifications, the British reintroduced clauses which provided that, in case Commonwealth trade was damaged by the loss of U.K. preferences, the Community must accept responsibility for putting things right.

The British had shown the draft, which amounted to twenty-four amendments, to their Dutch friends. The Dutch warned them that though the changes might be technically sound they were, in the present state of play, politically extravagant. But the objection was too late: the amendments were already being Roneoed for distribution at the conference.

From then on, until three o'clock on Saturday morning, and then again after breakfast, the Six quarrelled over their next move. Couve de Murville went back to the Baumgartner Plan and suggested that the conference should adjourn for a few months while the delegates considered it. All five of France's partners indignantly protested, and M. Couve this time gave in and agreed to go on. He added, however, that France had now reached the limit of its concessions.

Once again, as the British amendments were examined and all the substansive ones rejected, the Pope and the Emperor coordinated their strategy. Finally the French did accept one more concession: they agreed to a statement that 'the Community, in taking measures required to raise the income of those who work in agriculture inside the Community, and in perfecting the rational development of agricultural production, would also contribute to a harmonious development of world trade, ensuring a satisfactory level of exchanges between itself and third countries, including the countries of the Commonwealth'. (The British would have tagged on, after the word Commonwealth, the phrase 'which are present important suppliers of member states inside the enlarged Community in temperate food products'. This was never accepted and the argument was still pending when the negotiations collapsed.) At the time, nevertheless, the French concession was regarded as a major breakthrough, and on Saturday morning one French delegate said the revised document 'will still be a bitter pill, but I think the British will swallow it'. In fact they did not.

When the seven reconvened at about half past three on that

Saturday afternoon, hundreds of journalists, photographers, and radio reporters were converging at the *ad hoc* press room arranged on the ground floor. At 8 p.m. the Belgian Foreign Minister, his plump face wreathed in smiles, told the mob: 'I think we shall agree.'

M. Spaak was wrong. But although finally the failure to agree was between Britain and the Six, the real fight was between the five and France. It was during the last twenty-four hours that the French decided that, if the five were so keen on bringing Britain in, they must be made to pay the price. The price at this point was a firm commitment on the highly explosive issue of the financial regulations. This was a scheme designed to compel all the member states to pay, by 1970, into the Community chest the money they received from the levies the Community imposed on the import of foreign foodstuffs. This would mean that the big importing countries would pay a lot and that the money would probably be used to help subsidize the exporters: it was obviously immensely to France's advantage.

In principle the Six had already agreed to this plan in their package deal (without Britain) in January 1962. But they had framed the commitment in deliberately ambiguous terms.

The fact that the explosion occurred on the final night was partly Britain's fault. Most people in Brussels felt that if they had left the subject in decent obscurity until they came in the importing countries would have had their way. But the unfair sharing-out of the financial burden had already produced questions in the House of Commons. Heath himself had skirted the subject in February, leaving it to Sir Pierson Dixon to insist in May that Britain must know precisely the meaning of the January commitment.

Later, realizing they had opened up a most unpleasant Pandora box, the British tried to shut it up again by announcing that, anyway, they accepted the principle of the financial rules. But by now the French were beginning to suspect that once Britain was inside France was going to be very unfavourably sandwiched between two major importing countries. They therefore decided that agreement was essential in advance.

On Saturday night they told the Five that France would refuse the much debated pledge on Commonwealth agriculture unless the others agreed to a clarification of the financial rule. This, they insisted, must then be appended for ratification to the Treaty admitting Britain into the Community.

Robert Marjolin, the Commission's Vice-President, managed, during the night, to work out a plan which would have assured the Community of the revenues, but would no longer have made the ratification of this plan by the six Parliaments a condition of Britain's entry into E.E.C. The compromise was at first accepted with relief by the Six at 2.30 on Sunday morning. But a little later, when it was discovered that the British delegation still felt unable to go along, the Germans and Dutch changed their minds.

There was a further clash among the Six in Britain's absence when M. Spaak again raised the question of New Zealand:

M. COUVE: 'What obligations have we got towards the New Zealanders?'

M. SPAAK: 'The fact that twice in our lifetime their men have come over to be killed for freedom.'

M. COUVE: 'But their farmers are a great deal better off than our own, probably better off than anywhere in the world. Why are we pledged to do anything for them?'

M. SPAAK: 'Because we are sitting around this table organizing their ruin.'

As dawn broke on Sunday morning, the delegates, who had missed two nights' sleep, were beginning to wilt. The chairmanship had fallen to the stout and amiable Luxembourgeois Minister for Foreign Affairs and Wines, who, after summoning Heath to rejoin the Six, collapsed and had to be escorted out. Signor Colombo, who took his place, told Heath he was happy to say the Six now agreed on special treatment for New Zealand. Couve doodled and said nothing. (It was only the following October, when the minutes of the last meeting were submitted for approval, that he pointed out that it was inaccurate to say that an agreement had been reached. In the end he accepted the minutes but insisted on inserting a paragraph denying that the French were in any sense committed on New Zealand's behalf.)

As breakfast-time approached, the delegations were still arguing both on the text of a special statement on temperate foodstuffs, and about the financial regulations. At that point even the indomitable Colombo had to admit that further debate on this issue was a waste of time. He adjourned the negotiations until October.

Most of the continental participants still believe that British strategy was to hold out until after the Commonwealth Conference and that, despite the show of zeal, they did not therefore really want an agreement before the recess. This seems doubtful. But it is certainly true that Heath was earning himself the name of a sturdy fighter and that during that Saturday night and Sunday morning he effectively exposed charges held against him then and later by the Labour Party that he was 'negotiating on his knees'.

On the other hand, dissertations on what constituted 'a reasonable price policy' and arguments on the anticipated disposal of financial revenues eight and a half years away seemed to have little relevance to real life. In fact, before the meeting broke up, one of the keenest advocates of Britain's entry, the German State Secretary of Foreign Affairs, Rolf Lahr, called together a select group of British journalists and said he was quite sure that if only Britain would come in 'the commercial policies of the Community would not be so very different from those the British wanted'. Certainly he was right in thinking the balance of power would have been decisively different.

But the continentals' anxiety that agreement would be 'now or never' was not shared by the British leaders. On the contrary the British Government, after prolonged hesitations, was just preparing to build up the European commitment as the central plank in the Conservative Party platform for the next general election.

CHAPTER ELEVEN

`BRUSSELS: LAST ROUND

THERE was little time to lose. The Conservative Central Office had been given cruelly short warning of the Prime Minister's original European bid and had been slow in catching up. Even as late as July 1961, the very month in which the Prime Minister announced his decision, the *Conservative News Letter*, a private bulletin designed to keep local branches in line, was saying: 'The Liberals call on the Government to apply forthwith to join the Common Market. It is foolish advice which the Government are wise to reject.'

At the beginning of 1962, though no longer dismissing entry into Europe as foolish, the Central Office was still finding it an embarrassing kind of a cause. Indeed the Prime Minister himself had been unwilling to stake his reputation on a deal with Europe. He wanted to be sure whether the negotiations would succeed and he was also afraid perhaps that excessive eagerness might damage Heath's negotiating posture.

In this he was probably wrong. The continentals were more likely to underestimate than to exaggerate the degree of Britain's enthusiasm for Europe: and British caution did not necessarily encourage them to adopt a positive attitude.

This is the verdict of the most distinguished French economic writer, Pierre Drouin of *Le Monde*, in his book *Europe and the Common Market* (which should be compulsory reading for British ministers and officials before they take their next crack at the continent).

The parcelling-out of little concessions all through the exhausting negotiations was particularly ill received by the French delegates, as distrust had prevailed from the very outset over Britain's candidacy. Sulking ostentatiously, despite all the entreaties, during the initial installation of the Coal and Steel Pool, then over the Common Market and Euratom, underestimating the chance that these new institutions might work because incapable of believing in Franco-German reconciliation, trying unsuccessfully to create a free-trade organization, which would have killed the Common Market in the egg, setting up a European association to rival the Common Market, only to end up by knocking on the door of the Six, Great Britain could hardly be surprised if a certain suspicion surrounded this belated gesture.

Yet the Prime Minister still preferred to behave as if nothing special was happening. In his January 1962 Party broadcast and television appearance, he even managed to evade the subject altogether. A month later, the 'Gallery' television programme put on an investigation into the political implications of Britain's entry. Continental speakers explained that in the European view it would indeed mean a major break with Britain's past, and the transfer of large slabs of power from London to Brussels. Heath participated, but barely concealed his exasperated belief that, in the delicate state of the talks, certain explosive issues were better left untouched.

By the summer things had changed. Macmillan had had an unusually cordial reception from de Gaulle at the Château de Champs and found him surprisingly cooperative. Despite disturbing noises from overseas, Sandys was now confident that the Commonwealth would not erect any insuperable barriers. The President of the Brussels Commission himself, the stern and unyielding Professor Hallstein, was saying to anybody within earshot that the Brussels talks had reached the point of no return, and *must* not be allowed to fail.

And so, on 20 June, almost a year after his initial announcement, Macmillan made his first public speech stressing the political value of Britain's links with Europe and referred to the risk that she might become a poor little offshore island if she stayed out. Here was the first shot in the campaign designed to reach its climax at the annual Conservative Party Conference in October.

By this time, Macmillan had come to believe that Europe would be a good election issue and was hoping that Labour would oppose it. The Conservatives subsequently denied that they were trying to make political capital out of a decision effecting the destinies of Britain. Heath could truthfully say that in the summer of 1962 he was regularly briefing T.U.C. leaders on the state of the negotiations as well as those leaders of the Labour Party who would agree to come. These included George Brown but not Hugh Gaitskell.

Yet the Government never took up suggestions from outside the political parties that the whole vital topic should be dealt with on a bipartisan basis. The Prime Minister himself refused a proposal from Harold Wilson that a joint committee might examine the impact of entry on the House of Commons itself. There is no doubt that the Conservatives did want to make political capital out of entry, though this hardly proves the left-wing contention that the whole idea was no more than an electoral 'gimmick'.

The Conservative Party was itself divided. But the anti-marketeers never had the slightest hope of capturing the party, even if, as they were later to show, they could have a decisive nuisance value at the polls. As the official line hardened in favour of Europe, they retaliated by holding a number of meetings up and down the country, but they proved curiously unable to rally famous names. Most of the anti-marketeers were recruited from the same diehard, nationalist, and slightly discredited ranks as the Suez rebels, but of the two most prominent and powerful leaders of the 1956 rebellion, Julian Amery was now inside the Government and one of the keenest advocates of joining Europe, and the Marquis of Salisbury showed no signs of personal involvement either way. Eden, now Lord Avon, was by far the Government's most eminent opponent within the party ranks but, despite friendly overtures from Lord Beaverbrook, who was quite willing to make publicity and funds available, Mr Macmillan's predecessor, even had he desired to, would hardly have had the physical strength after his grave illnesses to go back into the fray.

While the Conservative Party thus moved nervously into full commitment to the Common Market, the Labour Party under Gaitskell was shifting the other way. In the summer of 1962 a head count by the *Economist* of the Parliamentary Labour Party produced eighty M.P.s against, seventy-five for, and the remaining hundred ready to follow their leader.

Gaitskell's personal position was therefore of crucial importance. It has been suggested that the Labour leader finally threw in his weight against the Common Market to appease his vociferous critics on the left: the doctrinaires and the neutralists. Certainly another head-on collision with them, on the scale of the Party battles on unilateralism and Clause 4, might have been fatal to the Party's survival. Suspicions that Gaitskell was being less than frank were encouraged by many months of subterfuge when he publicly argued that he favoured joining the European Community – but only on conditions on which it would have ceased to be a Community.

To the continentals, the essential difference between the new Community and traditional inter-governmental arrangements was that the Community involved the transference of powers of decision and action from a national to a central body. Yet until July 1962 – when a meeting of European socialists forced him into the open – Gaitskell cheerfully managed to present himself as being *for* the Common Market but *against* anything 'supra-national'.

When Gaitskell finally made up his mind to oppose the Macmillan bid, he did so after real anguish and despite strong pressure from his own friends in the Party. But once the decision was made, he threw himself with passion into the task of keeping Britain out. As leader of the Opposition he had no direct control over policy: but his status as the probable next Prime Minister gave him an influence both at home and abroad that finally enabled him to work, perhaps decisively, for Britain's exclusion.

No single man contributed more to Gaitskell's final resolve to fight the Government's Common Market decision than the brilliantly persuasive Indian Ambassador, B. K. Lall, accredited in Brussels, who came over in September 1962, in advance of the Commonwealth Prime Ministers conference. In private talks, which made a profound impression on the Labour leader and which Gaitskell frequently quoted back afterwards to his friends, Lall denounced the British negotiators for failing to get good enough terms for the undeveloped countries. But this did not prevent the Indians, after the rupture of the talks between E.E.C. and Britain five months later, from asking E.E.C. to consider reviving the plans for a comprehensive trade agreement between their country and the Six along precisely the plan originally worked out by the British negotiators.

Just before the Prime Ministers' conference began, Gaitskell organized a gathering of the socialist Commonwealth leaders. The meeting, afterwards described by members of the Government as 'a stab in the back', went on record opposing Britain's entry into E.E.C. on the terms so far agreed by the Government, and declared: 'They would have inevitably done great damage to many countries in the Commonwealth and, therefore, to the unity of the Commonwealth itself.' This funereal socialist prelude caused the non-Labour Commonwealth leaders to feel that they could not afford to appear less demanding on behalf of their own countrymen than their political rivals and certainly exacerbated hostility, intransigence, and distrust at the subsequent conference.

For the Prime Minister, the Commonwealth Conference was the great test. It opened – a self-consciously informal family gathering – at Marlborough House, a grimy red brick and stone building near St James's Park, former home of the widowed Queen Mary, on 12 September.

The meeting, attended by eleven independent plus seven dependent territories, had no constitutional status; its decisions were not binding even on the smallest of the newly independent West Indian islands. Yet it could have bound the Prime Minister of England hand and foot. Macmillan knew that unless he could get the green light from his colleagues, and at the very least prevent them from publicly proclaiming that Britain's entry into E.E.C. was incompatible with the survival of the Commonwealth, then it would be impossible to make his European bid politically acceptable either to his Party or to the British electorate.

Yet by now there was no question in the minds of those in power in Britain that the Commonwealth, whatever its political value, could offer no economic alternative to a link with Europe. On the contrary, it was more than anything the shrinking of Commonwealth markets, and the growing need to find outlets for British exports in the more industrialized countries, which had prompted the decision to apply for entry into Europe. In the previous year, for the first time in history, Britain had exported more to Western Europe than to the whole of the Commonwealth put together.

At Marlborough House, Macmillan himself opened the conference with a careful speech on which he and his advisers had worked for many weeks. His aim was to show that Britain's real choice was not between Europe and the Commonwealth, but between increasing her political and economic strength inside Europe, which would enable her to give adequate support for the Commonwealth, or staying out of Europe, going downhill, and being unable to help the Commonwealth at all.

It was Mr Diefenbaker, the Canadian Prime Minister, who the next day opened the heavy artillery against British positions. For the past few weeks Diefenbaker had been unusually silent, and only those close to him knew that for months he had been preparing himself for this great patriotic onslaught on the pusillanimous British Government for selling out the Commonwealth to foreigners. His critics said that his bravado was due to his flagging popularity at home and the need to rally public opinion by a fighting stance. (If this was his aim, it was unfulfilled. Within six months he had been succeeded by Mr Lester Pearson, a man known to agree with Macmillan that it would be very much better for Canada and the Commonwealth if Britain went in.) Diefenbaker's speech had been drafted well in advance and contained no reply to Macmillan's. He appeared not to the head but to the heart: a delegate from Ghana told the Queen at a royal reception a few days later: 'I was so moved I thought I was going to cry.'

Tuesday was a worrying day for the British ministers. Diefenbaker was followed by President Ayub Khan of Pakistan, who lashed out on European protectionism. He refused to give any credit to Heath's outstanding success in having obtained an admission from the Community that they must if Britain came in accept responsibility for ensuring that Pakistan, India, and Ceylon would be able to preserve and increase their earnings of European currencies.

Criticism from Ceylon and New Zealand was more restrained, but gloom thickened in the afternoon when Mr Nehru of India, looking frail, ancient, and miserable, prophesied that the Common Market would exacerbate world tension, increase the dangers of war, and, should Britain join, destroy the Commonwealth.

For the Africans, the Ghanaian delegates spoke first, denouncing the proposed association with the European Community as political servitude. This diatribe was expected: Ghana was going through a passionately anti-Western phase, and President Nkrumah himself had refused to attend the Conference. But what took the British Government unpleasantly by surprise was the discovery that even the friendly Africans were following Ghana's lead. So much so, indeed, that these widely believed and repeated a story of dubious origin which alleged that the British were planning to drag their hapless previous dependencies into the Community by the hair, as the entrance fee to the Common Market. Cabinet Ministers who had worked hard and long to overcome the Community's reluctance to extend to the Commonwealth Africans those same trading privileges and economic aid as the Six were committed to giving French-speaking Africa failed to conceive how anyone could credit such a ludicrous proposition. Here was a measure of the Government's total failure to explain to the Africans what they had been doing in Brussels – a failure which made it possible not only for the story to be believed, but for every one of the African countries flatly to reject the association offer.

But dissatisfied Africans were not likely to worry the Conservative Party. Their main anxiety was the veteran Commonwealth Leader Robert Menzies, Prime Minister of Australia and perhaps the only man with the authority and experience capable of rallying the conference into formal opposition. Menzies certainly distrusted his host, whom he held particularly responsible for the withdrawal of South Africa from the Commonwealth the previous year. He was particularly incensed with Sandys, who had visited him in 1961, issued with him a joint statement voicing Mr Menzies' apprehensions about the Common Market, and who had gone back to London saying that Menzies had really been much more cooperative in private and was only offensive in print for electoral purposes.

Menzies took the advantage of the weekend break in conference business to visit his old friend, Lord Avon, in Wiltshire, where he unburdened himself on the incalculable harm this Government was doing to the Commonwealth and the Conservative cause. Nevertheless, although his political situation at home – a majority of one seat, heavy reliance on the rural vote, and the prospect of an early election – counselled pugnacity, it was not Menzies' nature to lead a revolt of black and brown men against Britain. He knew too the acute American concern to see Britain inside the E.E.C. and sympathized with their purpose of strengthening Western power against the communist threat. Both Menzies and Mr Holyoak of New Zealand planned to stop off in Washington on their way home, and neither wanted to appear to the White House as wreckers.

Moreover, as Menzies and his battling Minister of Trade and Commerce, 'Black Jack' McEwen, well knew, if the Brussels terms were carried out Australia had much to gain. For years, the Australians had supported the French in demanding international commodity agreements and higher prices for wheat. They had been consistently opposed by Britain, and it was only in the course of the Brussels talks in June and July of 1962 that the British had come round to accepting the French view. Only such agreements could have released exporting countries (including Australia) from having to subsidize their wheat exports and so contribute to the upkeep of the importing countries.

Protestations continued to the end. Big sounding phrases such as 'The Treaty of Rome is like a surgeon's knife stuck into the body of the Commonwealth' (Sir Alexander Bustamente of Jamaica) quickly found their way into print.

But the Prime Minister, seconded by his pugnacious Secretary for Commonwealth Relations, fighting every inch of the way, managed in the end to avert the threatened disaster of a hostile communiqué or, worse still, no communiqué at all. The final statement, prepared under the dexterous management of the Secretary of the British Cabinet, Sir Norman Brook, was published on 18 September. Many Commonwealth criticisms were listed, but there was no demand for re-opening agreements already arrived at or for limiting Britain's freedom to take its own decision when the time came.

No one had pressed an earlier suggestion that the Prime Ministers should meet again to declare themselves on any final terms. Many of the Prime Ministers by this stage had been privately alarmed by the cumulative effect of so many hostile speeches, and some of them dreaded the demands which might be made on the Commonwealth, should the Brussels negotiations collapse.

And so the Government overcame what most people wrongly

thought would be their biggest hurdle into Europe. The Prime Minister was free to devote his attentions to the coming Party Conference and the next general election, and Heath could go back to Brussels without having to fear Commonwealth disavowal of the best bargains he could make.

Gaitskell, equally, could take some comfort: the speeches of the Asian, African, and old Dominion leaders had supported his thesis that the Commonwealth was in danger. At the Labour Party Conference in the Brighton Palladium early in October the line was still to suspend judgement until the final terms of entry into Europe were known. But now, for the first time, Gaitskell abandoned his pretence of waiting and seeing and instead revealed his oratorical talents: as he flung himself into a passionate denunciation of the entire European enterprise, these turned out to be a great deal more histrionic than most people had suspected.

He lightly dismissed the economic arguments: he said (inaccurately) that all the economists who had given the matter serious attention had agreed the case for going into the Common Market to be fifty–fifty. But the punch was not economic but political. Gaitskell's tone was fervently nationalist, outspokenly contemptuous of the 'two faces of Europe', and as reverential as the *Daily Express* towards Britain's duty to the Commonwealth. He forecast that Britain's entry into E.E.C. might be 'the end of Britain as an independent nation' and affirmed that as 'a province of Europe' Britain could obviously not remain the 'mother country' of a Commonwealth of Nations. He nostalgically recalled battles fought shoulder to shoulder with Commonwealth soldiers in the First World War (the French were presumably getting killed elsewhere) and foresaw that a decision to join E.E.C. 'would mark the end of a thousand years of history'.

This speech enchanted the neutralists and fellow-travellers in the Labour Party because it was hostile to any Western commitment. It was also tremendously popular with the rank and file. For once the mob was offered an outlet for herd loyalty, and a jingo sense of superiority to foreigners, which the Labour Party's non-conformist conscience normally forbids.

Watching from the press gallery upstairs I recalled a similar reinstatement of the hyphen between 'national' and 'socialist', a similar echo of a Nuremberg rally, in Toulouse, at a French socialist Congress just before the Fourth Republic collapsed. The issue there had been not Europe but Algeria, and the socialist leader, Guy Mollet, had made an impassioned, eloquent speech defining the French national case against the bandits of the F.L.N. Playing the patriotic theme, Mollet recalled that he personally had been a war orphan and sent his greetings to the soldiers fighting for France. Glowering behind him was the rotund figure of the fraternal delegate from Britain, Aneurin Bevan, attended by a young official from Transport House who was whispering a simultaneous translation in his ear. At the end, the hall rose to applaud and sing the 'Internationale'. Bevan stayed seated.

But as Gaitskell spoke in Brighton, many of my colleagues whose experience had been in England rather than abroad were thinking of Bevan in another context. They recalled that the last time the Party met in Brighton had been when Bevan had publicly renounced the unilateralists and joined Gaitskell in publicly committing himself to the Western alliance. In doing so he deserted and bitterly disappointed his closest followers who had fought for the Bevan cause so long, often at considerable political peril.

This time, it was the other way up. Gaitskell now was turning his back on the men who had stood by him in his time of trouble – George Brown, Ray Gunter, John Strachey, Frank Pakenham, Roy Jenkins, Desmond Donnelly, and others – who suddenly discovered themselves alone and deserted while the left-wingers and the unilateralists had captured their leader. After Gaitskell sat down, his oldest antagonist, the unilateralist boss of the giant Transport and General Workers' Union, Frank Cousins, rose to salute 'one of the finest speeches we shall ever hear'.

To Macmillan the Gaitskell assault could only come as a relief. Now that the Commonwealth challenge had been met, the European issue could provide the Conservative Party with the political ammunition they badly needed. The only challenge now could be from the Liberal Party. The Liberals had indeed been winning some spectacular bye-electoral successes, but with all the resources of the Conservative propaganda machine it did not turn out to be too difficult to steal the smaller party's European clothing.

Macmillan's first move was to issue a small pamphlet, with a picture of himself on the front, elaborating the views he had expressed at Marlborough House. He also saw to it that entry into the Common Market became the central issue at the Party's annual conference, thus practically obliterating all embarrassing domestic issues.

By the time the Party assembled on 10 October they were ecstatic. Europe was their cause and Macmillan their man of history. Young and not-so-young Tory delegates, eager, as the conference began, to line up on the side of Europe and progress, bought little 'Yes' badges on the promenade for sixpence each and wore them to shame the diehards. (This novelty was widely reported on the continent: I recall, with regret, having failed to fulfil a special request from a French diplomat who asked me to take a pocketful of badges to Brussels for the French delegation to wear at their next meeting.)

The Tory speeches at Llandudno repeated, but with a new flamboyance, the reasons why Britain would be better off inside than outside the Common Market. The anti-marketeers made some moving allusions to the Commonwealth; but there was no Ghanaian delegate to break down and weep. It was left to Mr Butler, now fully committed (though still, as Chairman of the inter-ministerial committee, restraining Mr Heath from too much flexibility on bacon and eggs at Brussels), to make the celebrated rejoinder to Gaitskell: 'For them, a thousand years of history. For us, the future!'

For the Conservatives, it was a cosy, heart-warming experience to feel that their side now was being internationalist and progressive – just as it had been a relief for the Labour rank-and-file to discover that for a change they could be the ones to cheer the flag, the Commonwealth, and the great traditions of England. The European issue had muddled things up.

Back in Brussels, the effect of the Commonwealth and Conservative conferences was to convince everyone that there was now nothing to prevent Britain from coming to terms. Macmillan's Cabinet, however, saw it differently: they felt they should put up a stern resistance to any continental assumption that the British position was softening up. The motive was political; at all costs nothing must be done to give credit to the Gaitskell charge that Heath was 'negotiating from his knees'. Even if this meant dragging the negotiations on until 1963, the Party would still have over a year to carry through the necessary legislation required by signing the Rome Treaty, and could still get the whole agreement ratified before the next general election.

On 8 October Heath returned to Brussels. While reassuring his colleagues that he would not go back on agreements so far reached, he none the less laid before them the principal demands made at Marlborough House. His initiative was partially successful. For the Africans he managed to obtain two important concessions: first, for the countries that did not want association, the Commission would be ready to negotiate a special trade agreement. Second, the Six agreed that in case the Commonwealth Africans changed their minds, as predicted by Duncan Sandys, the offer of association would remain.

For the Asians, Heath persuaded the Six that negotiations over trade agreements with India, Pakistan, and Ceylon should start immediately Britain entered the Common Market, though he failed to induce them to allow these countries to preserve their access to British markets until such negotiations were complete.

But what really brought what de Gaulle was later to call 'the lengthy Brussels negotiations' to a standstill were not Commonwealth exigencies but British domestic agriculture and more particularly bacon and eggs.

There had indeed been a certain hardening up on farm matters both in Brussels and in London during the summer recess. In Britain the farmers had been lobbying M.P.s, and Butler was firmly committed to their support. In Brussels, the Commission had been preoccupied throughout the summer with the Herculean task of implementing the new Community agricultural system and had hardly had a minute to read the relevant papers. When the Commissioners at last had time to examine Britain's plans for preserving, as much as possible and for as long as possible, the system of feather-bedding which had served the British farming community so well, they professed to be appalled.

The basic quarrel was not how European agriculture should be organized in the future: the Minister of Agriculture had already agreed that Britain would progressively move towards the Community system. The real dispute was over how to get there. Some British ministers were privately reassuring the farmers that by the end of a long-drawn-out transitional period there was every reason to expect that the Community system would anyway have shown itself unworkable. With this in mind, the British proposed to keep on the existing British system, and only gradually eliminate farm subsidies. The Six, on the contrary, wanted Britain to go over to the Community system immediately. Though they were ready to examine new systems of subsidies to prevent any excessive jerk in British prices, they wanted to strip the British farmer immediately of his guarantees. They objected to the British system, whereby the farmer was paid the difference between the guaranteed and the market price, because it eliminated any direct relation between the farmer's earnings and the current price level. They protested that this would encourage over-production. If Britain joined Europe, they argued, then British eggs and bacon would flood the Six, the British farmer would undersell his rivals, and the British Government would pick up the bill for the difference between the money he had obtained and the guaranteed price.

Dozens of variations in types of subsidy were examined, but no real progress was made before Christmas. On the British side the Ministry of Agriculture, under consistent pressure from the National Union of Farmers, counselled prudence.

On the continental side it was whispered, though this could never be proved, that there was a secret Franco–German deal. Under this, the Germans agreed to support the French on the subsidy argument, and in return the French backed the Germans against British plans to reduce the Community price for wheat. Weeks and months went by. Ministers were now meeting at fortnightly intervals and their officials almost uninterruptedly. But the sessions produced only peripheral agreements: association for Aden and Malta; the extension of the special arrangements agreed for Pakistan, India, and Ceylon to the Federation of Malaya; the abolition of tariffs for tinned kangaroo meat, fish-liver-oil, and tropical hardwoods.

Relations inside the Community went from bad to worse. The Dutch, now in the chair, made no attempt to conceal their support for British proposals; an attitude which the French regarded as treacherous. In most of the agricultural arguments France was represented by M. Pisani, the bearded and unusually outspoken Minister of Agriculture. Discussion around the conference table often plunged to well below diplomatic level.

To make matters worse, the French once again demanded that, before there could be any agreement on Britain's entry, the Five must accept the dreaded financial regulation for the exclusive benefit of France.

Nevertheless, the French attitude was by no means wholly negative. When the EFTA problem first came up, and Heath explained that the British considered themselves bound to remain outside the Community until arrangements had been made to look after their EFTA partners, it was Couve de Murville who, to Heath's great relief, suggested a stand-still agreement whereby Britain could come into E.E.C. without at first imposing tariffs against EFTA: this would give more time for the enlarged Community to come to terms with the other EFTA members.

The French also shifted from their insistence that Britain should abandon her deficiency payments system the day she entered the Common Market; they agreed instead that, in view of the British Government's pledges to the farming community, existing arrangements should be preserved for the duration of the present Parliament.

During most of this time, the Commission itself had done little to ease the agriculture deadlock. It was not until 12 December that Dr Sicco Mansholt moved back into the centre of the stage. Mansholt obtained a mandate to form a committee of inquiry to examine the effects of the various plans for adjusting British agriculture to the Community system and so, by implication, to point to possible solutions.

This committee soon ran into trouble. There was difficulty even in agreeing on such relatively simple facts as the prices received by British and Community farmers for given qualities of grain. It was not until 15 January, the day after the General's fatal press conference, that the committee was ready to submit its long technical report.

Behind the scenes, however, Dr Mansholt had been conducting

secret discussions with the British ministers in the convenient privacy of the Dutch delegation; there, certain deals, which have never hitherto been divulged, were already agreed. By these, the British farmer would have had to accept more flexible forms of subsidy for pig-meat and eggs than the existing system of deficiency payments, but until the end of 1970 he would still have got some form of governmental support. Compromises had also been reached on the projected level of cereal prices.

Mansholt was also hoping to get France's five partners to meet the French demand for extending the common agricultural policy to dairy-products, on which they had so far failed to agree, partly because the Italians and Dutch preferred to go on protecting oil and margarine against butter. In return, Mansholt thought the French would allow a duty-free quota of butter and cheese from New Zealand into the Community or British market.

All this, however, was in the secret files. Just how long the whole package deal would have taken to materialize, and whether in the end Soames would, as he hoped, have managed to sell it to the National Farmers Union, is, and must remain, a matter of conjecture. What is true, and can now be said, is that just before the General's 'No' Soames had sent a private message to Mr H. Woolley, the new head of N.F.U., asking whether he might happen to be free to come over to Brussels, perhaps at the end of the week, to give his advice on a possible package deal.

These gleams of hope, however, were visible only in the private smoke-filled rooms. From the formal minutes of meetings, it was impossible to challenge the General's assertion that negotiations on the important issues had been at a stand-still since October. Yet, to suggest that they had reached a point where further discussions were a waste of time was to fly in the face of facts well known not only to the little group of ministers and high officials involved in the secret negotiations, but also to hundreds of people – diplomats, Commission staff, secretaries, typists, journalists, lobbyists – who knew perfectly well that the General was wrong.

On the other hand, to go as far as the British Prime Minister, and to accuse the General of breaking things off just as the two sides were on the verge of agreement, is leaning too far the other way. Even supposing that some of the agricultural problems were

146

nearing solution (and since Mr Woolley had not arrived this is by no means certain), weighty issues still remained – the Commonwealth, tariffs on raw materials, arrangements for Britain's EFTA allies – on which hardly any work had been done. Finally, no effort had yet been made, except very secretly by senior members of the Brussels Commission, to work out the all-important question of the new political balance – national representation and weighted voting – which would be appropriate for the enlarged Community.

Even before the General's 'No', doubts were increasing in Brussels about whether there was the energy and will-power necessary to overcome the hurdles ahead. Certain senior members of the German Foreign Ministry still believe today that even without the veto no agreement would have been reached.

Macmillan told the House of Commons when it was all over 'that the French Government, in their hearts [why the plural?], had long feared success I do not doubt . . . but I think in all fairness the decision might have been taken a long time ago and not after fourteen months of negotiation.' He was right in saying that it was certainly not the state of the Brussels negotiations on 14 January 1963 which provoked the General's action. But history will surely decide that Macmillan also had his part in the final rupture. The long delay in starting the negotiations; the even longer delay in building up British confidence in the European venture; the absence of any firm political commitment until the Government seemed to face imminent electoral defeat; the stalling for so many weeks on how to subsidize bacon and eggs; the innate reluctance to take risks and trust foreigners – all these prepared the setting for the final disaster. Without them, the opportunity for the General's veto might never have arrived.

CHAPTER TWELVE

THE DÉBÂCLE

IT has been argued that General de Gaulle never intended to let Britain into Europe, and that the entire Common Market negotiation was from the beginning nothing more than a gigantic hoax.

This is the view of that stalwart advocate of British links with Europe, Lord Boothby, who believes that by the time the Government applied it was already too late. When it was all over, and having already abandoned the Conservative Party in disgust, he gave his account of the Government's European record:

There was [Britain's] fatal refusal to join the Coal and Steel Community; the equally fatal refusal to join E.E.C.; the implacable hostility of the late Ernest Bevin and the noble Earl, Lord Avon, to the Council of Europe and everything it stood for; and finally the refusal of Her Majesty's Government to take part in the negotiations which resulted in the Treaty of Rome, or to take the Common Market seriously until it had become a reality, and a most prosperous reality at that. By the time de Gaulle came to power, we had missed the boat.

Yet in the summer of 1962 things looked different. In Brussels, as we have seen, the French mission was seeking to secure the best possible terms for France in the event of Britain's entry; it was not trying to keep Britain out. After the Brussels summer meeting, Couve de Murville himself paid a visit to Oslo and told the Norwegian Government that he was assuming that Britain's entry was only a matter of time. In Paris, the new long-term plans for French agriculture, being drawn up by the Commissariat for Planning, were based on the assumption of an enlarged Common Market.

This was the informed French view. On Bastille Day, in July, the former French Prime Minister, Michel Debré, happened to be visiting London, and was walking to St James's Street with the new

French Ambassador, M. Geoffroi de Courcel, on their way to a party. Debré, though he had resigned, was a frequent visitor to de Gaulle at the Élysée; and de Courcel was one of the General's oldest associates – he had been on the R.A.F. aircraft which flew the General to England in June 1940. As they walked, the two men exchanged views; and discovered that each was convinced that Britain was now 'coming into Europe'.

As for de Gaulle himself, he seems to have come nearest to accepting Britain's entry after his long private meeting with the Prime Minister at the Château de Champs at the beginning of June.

At that stage, the problem weighing most heavily on the General's mind was the difficulty France was encountering with her bomb. At the end of the Algerian War in March 1962, the General had been left with a dangerously disgruntled professional army on his hands, deprived of its final *raison d'être*. As an army man himself he considered it of vital importance to revive the army's own sense of mission, or in his own words 'to re-integrate it into the nation'. For this purpose he felt it must be given the most modern weapons: a nuclear armoury was needed to salvage its loyalty and self-respect.

To the Americans, who were always perfectly ready to scrap and remodel their armed forces to meet the requirements of new military techniques, the idea of acquiring nuclear weapons for the sake of the soldiers was utterly incomprehensible. But there is no doubt that this was the key to the General's indomitable determination to make France nuclear.

Yet despite the most intense efforts, both in the production of nuclear explosives and in the task of building the aircraft and rockets to deliver them, progress was slow. France had started late; and every day the refusal of the Americans and British to share their nuclear knowledge became more irritating. As it stood, the French *force de frappe* only too obviously was open to the taunt by McNamara, the U.S. Secretary of Defence, that separate national deterrents were 'weak, ineffective, and prone to obsolescence'. Besides, the project was hideously expensive; one thousand million dollars were to be spent on the isotope separation plant alone – a device which was already being closed down in Britain because enriched uranium could be obtained more cheaply in

America. Still more irritating, tiresome deputies were beginning to ask questions in Parliament.

But on the credit side, there seemed definite signs that Britain was moving to the General's aid. Had not Macmillan himself, when M. Jean Chauvel called to take his leave as Ambassador to St James's, specifically referred to the logic of an Anglo–French nuclear partnership? Had there not been a series of *démarches* (no less than five, according to senior French officials) from Britons who could reasonably be taken to represent the government attitude, and had not all of them made it plain that Britain's decision 'to go into Europe' implied that Britain would be ready to extend its European policies to defence? And did not this in turn imply a nuclear partnership with France, the only other nuclear power in Europe?

Certainly, two cabinet ministers, Mr Thorneycroft, the Minister of Defence, and Mr Amery, Minister of Aviation, had indicated during their several official and private visits to Paris that they personally favoured moves in this direction. Both shared their French hosts' exasperation that Europe was being 'run' by the Americans.

All this was in the air when the two leaders met. But the extraordinary fact about their meeting is that although the British delegation expected the General to raise the question of nuclear cooperation, and although it was dominating the General's thinking, the subject was never discussed. Macmillan thought it wiser to keep quiet. The General himself was too proud to make a specific request for Britain's nuclear help, and thus place himself in the despicable role of *demandeur*.

Indeed, during the entire talk – as in others between these two men – it is doubtful whether there was ever any real meeting of minds. Neither asked for anything; and their mutual habit of speaking in generalities and surveying the world from Himalayan heights may well have led them to imagine themselves much closer than they really were. Afterwards, there was an encouraging official statement. It spoke of the 'community of interests' between Britain and France and of the need for this spirit to animate the Brussels negotiations. After Macmillan had left, the General, ruminating on changes in the world balance of power in the presence of one of his senior ministers, declared his astonishment at having discovered from his talks that the British really seemed determined to join the Community. Then he speculated on the prospects of an Anglo–French partnership which could redress the balance against the United States, and made it plain that he was thinking in terms of a concerted effort, particularly on the nuclear side. The General, clearly, had been left with the impression that the Prime Minister was now willing to move in this direction. As the Prime Minister outlined his European convictions and seemed to share the General's own dislike of being relegated by the Americans to second-class status, de Gaulle thought that perhaps, after all, Britain might be an asset in the kind of new Europe he wanted to create.

Later on, the General was to feel, bitterly, that the British had let him down. Yet it does not seem that there ever was any real breach of the line of policy laid down by the Prime Minister at the beginning of the Brussels negotiations. He had said then that there would be no question of asking the Americans to authorize a revision of the special 1958 arrangements, to benefit France, until after Britain was inside the Common Market. This was hinted at in Heath's opening speech to the Six, when he said: 'We in the U.K. will regard the successful conclusion of these negotiations as a point of departure, not as the end of the road.' Had Britain done otherwise – had she tried to swop nuclear help for the French in return for a ticket into Europe – she would have risked her 'special relationship' with the U.S., and might still have failed to get a new one in Europe; she would have been in danger, as a British cabinet minister put it, of 'falling between two stools'.

As time drew on, it became increasingly obvious to de Gaulle that despite public speeches and private reassurances about Britain's conversion to Europe, and about the need for a powerful European union capable of holding its own among the world giants, the British Government had no intention of loosening its transatlantic links. The General was certainly pleased with the Anglo–French arrangement for the joint development of a supersonic aircraft; but he began to fear the worst when this was not taken as a model for extending the partnership to missiles and nuclear weapons.

A month after the Château de Champs meeting, there was more depressing news for de Gaulle. On American Independence Day, 4 July, President Kennedy put forward his Grand Design of interdependence between the United States and an enlarged European Community. To Macmillan, who had said very much the same thing the previous year, this was highly gratifying. To de Gaulle, whose whole purpose in creating Europe was to throw off American shackles, it was the exact opposite.

For the one area in which de Gaulle so badly needed partnership – in building a nuclear force – was precisely the area where Kennedy's 'two-pillar' theory of the Atlantic partnership broke down. Some American visitors, coming over to Europe after the President's speech, hinted that the Americans were now more sympathetic to the idea of a 'European deterrent'.

In the late autumn, President Kennedy's influential adviser, Mr MacGeorge Bundy, visited Bonn and said, at a dinner party given by the United States Ambassador, Mr Dowling, and attended by a number of German officials, that he personally could not believe that 'the great nations of Europe will permanently stay outside the nuclear adventure'.

Yet official American policy still laid it down that though the Atlantic partnership must be founded on two pillars only one of them – the American not the European – should be nuclear.

Thus, paradoxically, it was probably Kennedy's own enthusiasm for Britain's entry into E.E.C. and his doctrine of Atlantic partnership which, more than anything else, contributed to the Brussels rupture. It convinced the General that he had been right all along and that Britain was, after all, incurably 'Anglo-Saxon'. The French were given an additional cause for grievance in September, when the Under-Secretary of Defence, Mr Gilpatrick, visited Paris to discuss American proposals for making nuclear submarines available to France. Three weeks later another message arrived: the Pentagon had changed its mind.

But although the Americans were holding back with their nuclear weapons they were driving ahead with other aspects of transatlantic partnership which, from the General's point of view, only made things worse. The Kennedy response to the Common Market had been the Trade Expansion Act, which authorized the

President to dismantle U.S. tariffs in order to encourage a freer transatlantic flow of trade. But de Gaulle's advisers and supporters – and here the General was assiduously backed by French industry – felt that American economic penetration of France was already excessive. French firms, it was argued, were far too small and too weak to be able to withstand American competition. When, in the autumn, Remington closed their French factory, and dismissed French workers, a major anti-American campaign was launched against 'dollar imperialism'.

In November French anxiety about American 'penetration' was sharply exacerbated by the unsolicited visit of Mr Orveille Freeman, the U.S. Secretary of Agriculture. Freeman publicly berated the Community's agricultural system, of which France was the main beneficiary, as 'regressive' and a menace to world trade. His French opposite number Edgar Pisani told me afterwards he did wish *le père Freeman* would stop claiming a divine right to dispose of American food surpluses in an area which, with the French technological revolution in full swing, was rapidly acquiring surpluses of its own.

Turning the knife in the wound, President Kennedy himself formally announced that the Americans would not reduce their high tariffs on industrial products unless they were compensated in agriculture: forty per cent of American exports to Europe were in foodstuffs and it was not a market the Americans were ready to abandon. To France, it seemed inevitable that if Britain were admitted into E.E.C. she would use all her influence to support France's less protectionist partners, notably West Germany and Holland, to give President Kennedy satisfaction.

The Cuba crisis, too, hardened the General's resolve. The Europeans almost unanimously objected to the unilateral American action in imposing a naval blockade and risking war; the French, to everyone's astonishment, were the only delegation at Nato which uncompromisingly supported the American action. But the General felt that Cuba proved his point: under duress, the Americans would always act independently. Europeans must learn to do likewise.

Meanwhile, as the General's doubts about the Anglo-Saxons had been increasing, so he had been moving closer to West

Germany. Outwardly, it might seem illogical that the General should judge Britain so harshly for being too close to the United States and yet base his foreign policy on increasingly intimate links with the Federal Republic. Germany wanted to stay occupied by American troops, and showed every sign of wanting to snuggle as closely as possible under the American nuclear umbrella.

But the General had always believed that, if he could unite Europe, France would emerge as the natural leader; and in Chancellor Adenauer he could have had no more fervent disciple. And Adenauer too was increasingly disenchanted with Washington. He had dearly loved and trusted John Foster Dulles: he was not the least surprised when former-President Eisenhower, visiting Bonn in August, told him that when *he* was in the White House they never took a major foreign policy decision without Dulles first saying: 'Let's see what Adenauer thinks.'

But the brash new young administration had never established similar links and the old Chancellor harboured a private conviction that a man like Kennedy, whose sister-in-law had married a Polish nobleman, was anyway likely to be anti-German. Basically, therefore, Adenauer was highly receptive to the General's argument that the Americans might do a deal with the Russians at the expense of Europe – and more particularly at the expense of Germany. Relations did not improve when the Chancellor tried to force the Americans to mend their ways by leaking to the press, in the Spring of 1962, the secret plans the Americans had elaborated for international access routes to Berlin; or again in telling the press, after Cuba, that Kennedy was being diddled by Khrushchev.

It had not been the General's original plan to base his whole European Union exclusively on the Germans. His earlier idea had been to form a loose political confederation of the six member states of the community to which Britain, if it behaved, might later be admitted.

The first definite move in this direction had been in July 1961, when the Six held a Summit Conference and agreed they should form a political union. The work of drafting a statute was entrusted to a committee presided over by a fervent Gaullist and former minister, Christian Fouchet. The difficulty was that all France's partners wanted some federal or supranational structure on the model of the E.E.C., whereas the General insisted that executive power must be exclusively reserved for the separate states.

For many months that winter, the diplomats had painstakingly worked on the discordant texts. Finally, they thought they had found an acceptable compromise. Then, in February 1962, the General, who had lost touch with what they were doing, suddenly looked at the papers and tore them up. French diplomats cite this episode as a classic example of *le jupitérisme*, government by thunderbolt, which de Gaulle was to exercise with such devastating consequences, a year later, against England.

Negotiations were therefore in a somewhat delicate state when, in April, Mr Heath plunged in and asked whether it might not be better if Britain, as a candidate member of the Common Market, participated also in the political talks? Belgium and Holland agreed: if they could not have their federal union, they would only accept the looser structure, with Britain inside to hold the balance against France.

To advisers who pointed out to him that he had now really antagonized Benelux, the General replied: 'Never mind! The British have been fighting for those little countries for a hundred years. They can have them.'

Then in July, Adenauer went on a French tour and saw de Gaulle. The two men agreed to suggest to the Italians that, since the Six-power community was evidently stalled, they might consider a three-power nucleus for the new Europe. The French prepared a text which German diplomats remember being shown during a military parade at Mourmelon. But 'Fralit' (France, Allemagne, Italia), as it came to be called, under prospective Franco–German hegemony, had very little appeal for the Italian Government, engaged at the time in the 'opening to the left'. And so finally the General and the Chancellor had nothing left but each other.

Perhaps they enjoyed it. The return visit de Gaulle paid to Germany at the beginning of September confirmed his convictions that France's future lay with the Germans rather than with the British. Here, at least, he could see that French leadership would not be contested. Young German liberals now claim that the whole visit was a professionally organized publicity stunt: it is certainly true that the French made elaborate advance preparations and that in Bonn the Federal authorities sent out police cars with loudspeakers announcing that the General was coming and urging the citizens to go out and cheer. But, whatever the reasons, the tour was a triumph. When, at Munich, the General stretched out his long arms and said, in German but with a marked French accent: '*Sie sind ein grosses Volk!*' reporters agreed they had not seen such explosions of enthusiasm since Hitler's day. But for the Brussels negotiations, the visit boded no good. Wherever de Gaulle went, he eulogized European culture as a purely continental phenomenon: referring to the great inheritance of Dante, Racine, and Goethe and slyly omitting references to Shakespeare.

The General came home in high good humour. He and the Chancellor had agreed to work out plans for institutionalizing Franco–German cooperation. The system, which envisaged regular meetings of political leaders and permanent committees of officials to coordinate foreign policy, defence, culture, and economics, was very similar to the confederal plan he had first suggested for the Six.

Two other influences were at work on the General, impelling him towards his 'No'. First, he became convinced that Macmillan was on the way out – hardly worth negotiating with. Soon after the shattering Conservative setbacks at the November bye-elections, Gaitskell, now prospective prime minister, visited Paris and revealed overwhelming hostility to the whole European project. Gaitskell also indicated that if the Labour Party came in they might be willing to examine arrangements with E.E.C. which fell short of full membership. The report which the General received from his Premier, M. Pompidou (he preferred not to see Gaitskell himself), convinced him that there was not going to be as much pressure for Britain's entry as he had expected.

Second, as Macmillan went down, the General went up. It is sometimes thought that the General was omnipotent from the very day he returned to power, having been, as the Gaullist propagandists subsequently made out, swept back into office by a popular disavowal of the Fourth Republic. But it is worth recalling that in a public opinion poll, taken shortly before the 1958 uprising, in which the French people were asked who they would like as leader, the General came far below the better-known dignitaries of the Fourth Republic: Antoine Pinay (conservative), Guy Mollet (socialist), Maurice Thorez (communist), and even the left-wing radical, Pierre Mendès-France, though by then the latter was already in political decline.

What really destroyed the Fourth Republic had not been a popular verdict, but a revolt of soldiers and policemen against the processes of 'decolonization' imposed by succeeding governments. The withdrawal from North Africa was ultimately inevitable, but de Gaulle was brought back by people who deceived themselves into thinking he could be their King Canute, holding back the waves of nationalism in North Africa.

During the four years in which de Gaulle gradually inched his initial backers towards hauling down the tricolor in Algeria, he still required the support of the moderate elements of the outgoing régime. But after the Algerian war was over (and it lasted more years under the Fifth than under the Fourth Republic), the General's authority was well established. His monopoly of radio and television helped his followers win an absolute majority in the November elections. Although the surviving representatives of the old republican parties in the National Assembly, socialist, radical and conservatives, were later all to speak out in the strongest possible terms against the Brussels rupture, by the end of 1962 they had ceased to matter.

It was thus a triumphant general whom Macmillan met when he arrived on Saturday morning, 15 December, on a bleak wet day at Rambouillet, where he had a gun thrust into his hand and was told to go shooting. In the afternoon, when the Prime Minister was allowed to come in and get dry and join his host by the fire, the imminent disaster was not yet apparent. They exchanged views on the international situation since Cuba, noted the American inclination to pay less attention to their allies, agreed on the great significance of the Chinese–Russian dispute, and expressed satisfaction over the useful Anglo–French deal on the supersonic aircraft. But when their advisers were called in, and they got down to discussing Britain's entry into the Common Market, an increasingly downcast and alarmed Macmillan had to listen to a long monologue on the reasons why the General had come round to the conclusion that Britain was not fit to become a full and loyal member of E.E.C. Why ever didn't you say so before? the Prime Minister protested. The General saw no need to reply.

Some French officials who have seen the French account of the talk, and have discussed it with the General, allege that the General was privately hoping that the Prime Minister would take up his arguments and refute them. He would have liked to hear Macmillan proving that, on the contrary, Britain was truly European – perhaps even so European as to be ready for a nuclear arrangement with France. De Gaulle was, as they put it, 'holding out a perch' on which he hoped Macmillan would alight.

But the group around the Prime Minister received no such impression. It was a cold dreary meeting. The General had not said anything about an actual rupture of negotiations and might have just been venting his ill-humour, as the Prime Minister devoutly hoped. It was not a good omen for the marathon meeting on Britain's entry due to start in Brussels early the following month, but the despatch which shortly went out to diplomats from Admiralty House indicated that the Prime Minister had not yet lost heart.

The evening after Macmillan's visit the General, still at Rambouillet, invited some of his ministers to dine. One of them, sitting next to him, said he wondered whether nuclear weapons had been discussed? 'No,' was de Gaulle's reply, 'we hardly mentioned them. It looks as if the best area of Anglo–French cooperation will be in aircraft and rockets.'

A few days afterwards, one of the senior French negotiators at Brussels took soundings. 'Well,' he asked one of the General's staff, 'did you get your famous nuclear weapons, and sell the pass at Brussels?' Again the answer was no, there had been nothing nuclear at all.

(The official, recounting the episode afterwards, conceded that as far as he was concerned had a nuclear deal been arranged he would have been delighted to go and plead the opposite case at Brussels. He was well enough versed in the voluminous files to have been equally well qualified to plead either that the negotiations were deadlocked and must be stopped, or, on the contrary, that they were making such progress that they should now be carried through to speedy conclusion.)

And so Macmillan went to Nassau to meet Kennedy. There, in return for American Polaris missiles, the British agreed to place their nuclear force, not within a European, but within a Nato grouping – presumably under American command. The deal was arranged without consulting de Gaulle.

Ostensibly, it might seem odd that such a crucial issue, directly affecting European military security, could have been elaborated without as much as an if-you-please to the President of France, who also happened to be a General and punctilious on points of national honour. Letters were sent from Nassau to tell him what was going on, but they made matters worse: they contained nothing more than the General had already read in the newspapers. It was a strange way to treat a man widely known to suffer from an acute persecution mania, amounting almost to paranoia, about the 'Anglo-Saxons'.

The reason for this conduct was not in the least conspiratorial. On the American side, as I had been told by State Department officials in Washington in November, the White House had given firm orders that there must be no new planning on the reorganization of the Nato command, or on a European nuclear deterrent, until *after* the completion of the Brussels negotiations. This policy was upset purely by the American budgetary calendar. The coming year's expenditures were being worked out: the decision to cancel Skybolt, on which Britain was counting, could no longer be deferred. Here was an immense enterprise, involving some two thousand million dollars, and if left on the books it would mean either that other lines of production, judged imperative by the Pentagon, would have to be deferred; or else that the budget would be inacceptably swollen.

The Americans knew that if they could not deliver Skybolt the British were going to ask for Polaris, and the man responsible for American defence, Robert McNamara, was certainly not going to allow this precious vehicle to be used, except as part of his own global strategy. The domineering former chairman of Ford's Motor Company, whose word on defence matters was law, had no time for the niceties of European politics. If Britain wanted

Polaris, all right. But the price must be the merger of the British force into a multilateral Nato grouping, under single American command. They could take it or leave it.

But Mr Macmillan could not – or thought he could not – leave it. He had had trouble enough with the Conservative Party, overcoming backbench resistance to his European initiative: he could not now come home and tell them that Britain had also lost her national deterrent. He felt, as one of the officials who accompanied him to Nassau said, that the Party simply would not take it.

As de Gaulle rightly suspected, when he heard what was afoot, the Prime Minister had been thinking in terms of a multilateral solution for the Polaris deal long before the Rambouillet meeting, but as Macmillan was not sure that the General would like it, he thought it better to get the agreement first and smooth things over afterwards. The compensation was to have been the offer of Polaris missiles to de Gaulle himself. This involved a change of U.S. policy: previously the Americans had held as basic doctrine that they should concede nothing to the French which they withheld from the Germans; otherwise the Germans might lose heart. But on this occasion Kennedy allowed an exception: and the Prime Minister half expected the General to be pleased.

Just before the President and the Prime Minister signed the final agreement one of the Americans present asked Macmillan whether he did not think this deal might compromise the all-important Brussels negotiations. 'Oh no,' said the Prime Minister, 'it has nothing to do with them.' But this was not the General's view.

After the Rambouillet encounter with Macmillan, the General had taken off for his own country house at Colombey-les-deux-Églises. Visitors were forbidden as he preferred to be left alone to plan the destinies of France. The two questions requiring immediate decision were Nassau and the Brussels talks. To this day, Dr Adenauer and many other continentals are convinced that Nassau made him so furious that he promptly decided on the Brussels rupture. But this is an over-simplification. De Gaulle's first reaction was hurt pride, but then, on thinking the situation over, he could see that for the first time, with the offer of Polaris, the American and British had in effect admitted France into their nuclear club. Early in the new year – weeks after Nassau – he had still not told his diplomats how to react.

On 2 January, he was back in Paris, and the British Ambassador, Sir Pierson Dixon, called to try and assuage his wounded feelings. The meeting was indecisive. Two days later Dixon was followed by the American Ambassador, Mr Charles Bohlen, who pointed out that the Polaris offer was only a starting point; the President would be pleased to consider the General's views. Bohlen left the Élysée with the impression that the General had not yet made up his mind.

Then five days afterwards, on 9 January, President Kennedy's special envoy, Mr George Ball, arrived to explain the plan to Nato. Now the emphasis shifted from what the Americans could do for France to what they could do for all Nato countries by a multilateral and integrated Western deterrent. The General sensed a roundabout way of bringing his own prospective *force de frappe* under American management. Two days later, and three days before the memorable press conference, the American Ambassador learnt privately that the Nassau deal was off.

But although the General had returned from Colombey without having finally made up his mind on the Polaris offer, he was already determined to veto Britain's entry into the Common Market. In his televised New Year message he regretted that Britain was not showing itself sufficiently 'European' to qualify for Common Market membership and looked forward to some future day when '*une* Angleterre' (not *l'*Angleterre which now exists) might evolve sufficiently to become acceptable.

At the first 1963 cabinet meeting, on 9 January, his ministers learnt how much his mind had hardened against continuing the Brussels talks. He conceded that by opposing Britain France risked being isolated but he anticipated that this would also be true if France continued the discussions, since the other five now seemed ready to make almost any concessions to precipitate Britain's entry. Britain, he told his ministers, was not ready to join as an effective partner. She would come in only for the purpose of opening up the Community to American penetration. (It seems that the General did not himself use the phrase 'Trojan horse' to describe Britain's entry into Europe as an American instrument;

the metaphor was conveyed to journalists by his minister for information, M. Alain Peyrefitte.)

After the General had spoken, several ministers intervened, not to question his view that Britain should be excluded, but to point to the diplomatic liabilities for France of taking responsibility for the rupture. The General listened in silence. When the ministers filed out they still did not know if he had been persuaded. Couve de Murville, who had been among those expressing alarm, thought afterwards the General might still decide to soften his attitude. But one of the old hands, who had been with de Gaulle right through the war, said that he knew his General well enough to know that he had irrevocably made up his mind.

Two days later, alarmed by press leakages on the General's intentions, Heath himself came to Paris to lunch with Couve, and asked him flatly whether or not, if agreement could be reached, the General would exercise a political veto? The French foreign minister hedged. Then, when Heath repeated the question, he replied that if the technical difficulties could be overcome 'no power on earth could prevent you from coming in'. Heath came back to London convinced that, however difficult the next few weeks were going to be, he could at least discount the dangers of a political veto.

The opposite was true. At his press conference the following Monday, de Gaulle did not specifically announce his intention of ordering his ministers to break off the negotiations, but he made it very clear indeed that he no longer regarded Britain as a candidate for admission.

Asked to define France's attitude to Britain's entry into the Common Market, the General started by emphasizing the community of interests binding the Six, noting that the French had rightly insisted that agriculture as well as industry must be merged. 'At this point', he went on, 'Britain put forward its candidature. It did so after having formerly refused to join in the Community while it was being built, after creating a kind of free-trade arrangement with six other countries and – I might as well say so, as everyone remembers it – after having applied pressure on the Six to prevent them from implementing the Common Market Treaty.

'This confronts Britain and the Six with an immense problem.

Britain is, in fact, insular and maritime, linked by her trade, her markets, and her supply routes to very varied and often very remote countries. She is entirely industrial and commercial: hardly agricultural at all.

'In her daily life, her habits and traditions are very special and very original. In short, the structure and present condition of England are widely different from those on the continent.

'How can things be arranged so that Britain, living, producing, and trading as she does, can still be incorporated into the Common Market as the latter has been conceived and functions? For example, the method by which Britain receives her food supply, which is to import supplies bought at the lowest prices from the two Americas and the old Dominions, while at the same time giving big subsidies to the peasants in England, is obviously incompatible with the system which the Six have naturally established among themselves.

'The system practised by the Six is to create a single market inside the community, fixing and subsidizing prices, organizing competition, and compelling each participant to pay into the central fund any economies it may make by buying its supplies from the outside market instead of inside the community.'

(A French official commented afterwards that this was about the best definition of the much-disputed financial regulation he had ever heard.)

'Once again then, how can Britain, being what she is, come into our system? It might have been thought that our English friends, in proposing their entry, had agreed to transform themselves to the point where they could apply all the required conditions.

'The question today is whether they can accept coming inside a single tariff wall, renouncing all preferences for the Commonwealth, abandoning any privileges for their own farmers, and repudiating the pledges they made to their EFTA partners. This is the real question.

'It cannot be said that at the present time Britain is ready to do these things. Will she ever be? To that question only Britain can reply.'

The General then forecast that if Britain came in, followed by the other applicants, the Community would lose its cohesion and fall prey to 'a colossal Atlantic grouping, under American dependence and control' which would soon swallow it up.

The General suggested that Britain should accept instead an association with the Common Market. Franco–British cooperation should continue, notably in science, technology, and industry.

The verdict was clear: the General was shutting Britain out.

The risk that he might do so, after allowing negotiations to drag on so long, had been worrying the Quai d'Orsay for some time. A senior official had earlier gone to the length of having a private chat with the General, in which he told de Gaulle an anecdote of obvious relevance:

Two neighbouring farmers wanted to marry off their son and daughter. The courtship had been going on for some time without results when the boy's family intervened to ask him to make up his mind. He said he could not decide until he had seen her without her clothes on. Aghast, the two families consulted and finally arranged that he should look through the keyhole while she was taking her bath. The ordeal lasted for some time while the families waited downstairs. Finally the boy came down: 'No,' he said, 'I never like girls with blue eyes.'

In the long negotiations in Brussels the General had had Britain stripped: now he was saying she could not come in because she was an island.

Despite the clarity of the General's pronouncement, neither the French nor other European ministers believed that he was going to break off the talks at once. The day after the Press conference, the Swedish Prime Minister, then visiting Paris, called at the Quai d'Orsay, and Couve indicated that the negotiations could be expected to last another couple of months.

In Brussels, the General's press conference had coincided with the beginning of what was supposed to be a great marathon session, providing the opportunity for some major package deal.

While the ministers were sitting round the grey steel rectangular table they had come to know so well, junior staff members had their radios on, and little slips of paper began to be handed in from the door to the various ministers. Eyebrows were raised, breath was caught, but nobody mentioned the General.

In Washington, it was early morning when the story broke.

There it was less what the General had said about Britain's European shortcomings than his charges against the U.S. which provoked eruptions. The General was publicly asserting that the U.S. guarantees to Europe were valueless:

'Who can say what tomorrow will bring? Who can say if, in the future, the political background having changed completely – that is something which has happened on earth – the two powers (the U.S. and the U.S.S.R.) having the nuclear monopoly will not agree to divide the world?

'Who can say that, if the occasion arises, the two, while each deciding not to launch its missiles at the main enemy so that it should itself be spared, will not crush the others? It is possible to imagine that on some awful day Western Europe might be wiped out from Moscow, and Central Europe from Washington. And who can even then say that the two rivals, after I know not what social political upheavals, will not unite?'

A young British defence department official, sent over with a team of experts to study the application of the Nassau agreement, recalls that he had a number of appointments that day at the Pentagon: 'It was no good at all. I never even mentioned the General, but every official I visited brought the subject up, hit the ceiling, and I just had to move on.'

The first European reaction to the General's performance was simply that it was too bad to be true: he could not really have meant it. Everybody went on as if nothing had happened. That night in Brussels, the ministers of agriculture, still struggling with the Mansholt fact-finding report and arguing about such highly controversial issues as how much British wheat goes into a British hen laying a British egg, sat up till 4.30 a.m. to get an agreed text. One of the men who sacrificed a night's sleep in vain was French minister, Edgar Pisani. Not that he, personally, expected de Gaulle would let Britain in: as he told his colleagues, no cock likes sharing his hens, not even if the other cock brings in six more hens (the EFTA partners) of his own.

On Tuesday the sense of imminent disaster brought people closer together. An interpreter who sat through the entire proceedings remembered it afterwards as 'an Indian summer'.

Paul-Henri Spaak suggested getting some difficult subject

formally agreed so as to demonstrate the falsity of the General's statement that negotiations were at a standstill.

After a private meeting with Heath the stage was set for a dramatic afternoon meeting. For the first time, Heath then agreed that, provided the conditions for adjusting British agriculture were satisfactory, he would accept the 1970 deadline for the ending of the transitional period. This was of symbolic significance to the Six: it was supposed to be then that the Common Market came to full fruition.

On Wednesday, the conference moved on to the tariffs, and Heath came forward with new package proposals. The Six met on their own in the afternoon to try and agree on their answer. Their meeting was interrupted by the arrival of M. Couve, coming straight from a cabinet meeting that morning in Paris where he had received the General's final instructions. He took his seat looking remarkably pale. Was it because the Paris–Brussels flight had been unusually bumpy, one ambassador whispered to his neighbour, or was it the agony of being cast as First Murderer?

As the argument got bogged down in lead and zinc, Couve signalled to his old friend Dr Luns, the Dutch foreign minister, whom he had been meeting in different parts of the world for the past twelve years. The two men went out together and the French foreign minister unburdened himself: 'We cannot', he said, 'go on with all this nonsense. I think we should call a special conference to arrange for the adjournment of the British negotiations.'

Luns protested that on the contrary the negotiations were making progress, that his Government was totally committed to Britain's entry, and that if France was too intransigent the whole Community might fall apart. Couve said he knew France was being criticized on all sides and he certainly could not allow France to be treated as 'an accused in the dock'.

The two men then called the Belgian chairman, M. Fayat, out of the meeting. He returned to announce that his French colleague was asking for a special meeting of ministers only to discuss 'organizing' (a French euphemism for disorganizing, a British delegate said later) conference business.

That night, at a dinner given for the seven ministers by their Belgian hosts, Heath learnt Couve's intention. He hurried back to hold a private delegation conference in the hotel. Then he telephoned the Prime Minister: 'hang on' was the advice he was seeking, and Macmillan agreed.

By Thursday, tension was extremely high. Only the ministers were admitted to the meeting, and the seventh floor was crowded with senior officials who could not get on with any useful work until they knew what the French would do. It was now that the French managed to get into the psychological pipeline their story of the secret protocols. Within a matter of minutes senior diplomats who should have known better were whispering to each other the news: Couve had arrived with evidence that besides the public Nassau communiqué the British and American leaders had made a secret deal of far-reaching political significance: among other things it would open up Berlin to the Russians and Africa to the Americans.

The next day the story appeared 'from normally well-informed sources' in the pro-French Belgian Catholic press. The day after that, the U.S. Embassy in Brussels issued an official denial. The week later, speaking at Liverpool, the Prime Minister himself found it expedient to say publicly: 'The rumours about a secret deal at Nassau are false.'

In the conference room, Couve never even mentioned Nassau. He concentrated his whole attack on the points still under dispute at Brussels, alleging that they were insurmountable and that consequently the negotiations were a waste of time.

The rumpus was indescribable. All the ministers lost their tempers, none with more zest than M. Spaak. Gone was the time when the Italians tried to act as intermediaries. The seventy-year old deputy Prime Minister, Attilio Piccioni, threatened to block France on every other issue unless the French gave in: if no Britain, then no financial regulation, no agreement on dairy farming, no signature of the association agreements for providing aid and trade to France's previous protectorates, and no special protocol for the newly independent Algeria.

While this uproar was going on Heath and his team were sitting in their little delegation office on the seventh floor. Continental friends were slipping in to keep them posted on what was happening. The biggest relief was to find the Germans standing firm. Schroeder had flown to Bonn for a special cabinet meeting and was now back in Brussels strongly attacking Couve's arguments.

Everywhere in Brussels, London, and Washington it was now felt that only the Germans could save the situation. Franco–German rapprochement was a cardinal point of the General's policy and in the following week Chancellor Adenauer himself was expected in Paris to sign the new Franco–German treaty.

For France, the worst shock was to be deserted by the Commission. When the Six had met to hear Couve's case, there had been an argument about whether Hallstein should participate. The five were afraid he would excuse French intransigence and might even agree with the General's contention that Britain was not truly European. The French insisted on his presence. But their calculations had gone wrong: the Pope was no longer on the Emperor's side.

Both Hallstein and Marjolin regarded the General's performance as a possibly fatal blow to the Community. Hallstein took the floor to point out that, as guardian of the Rome Treaty, he had to recall that it specifically left the Community open to new members. The Commission, he said, could not associate itself with a rupture of the British negotiations.

His severity may have been strengthened by a lightening private visit made by Jean Monnet the previous day. Monnet had been adamant: better no Europe at all than the kind of third-force military bloc the General envisaged.

That night Pisani flew back to Paris to report on France's total isolation, and Couve sent all his staff out of the office before putting through a private call – it was presumed to the Élysée. The French Ministers managed to obtain permission from de Gaulle to accept their colleagues' demand that the decision to break off negotiations should be postponed until the next ministerial session, scheduled for 28 January.

The news flashed round Brussels at once: ministers and diplomats began to feel that at the foot of the gallows they had received a last-minute reprieve. The French had yielded – and next week de Gaulle would be facing German pressure. By the time the Seven reconvened at the end of the month things might look different. If not, the General must understand he was not the dictator of Europe; the Five and Britain would go on without him. The mood was a mixture of hope and defiance.

But it was not shared by Chancellor Adenauer, who was due to leave forty-eight hours later on a visit to de Gaulle to sign the Franco–German 'treaty of cooperation and friendship'.

Whether or not he could at this late stage have deflected the General from his course remains doubtful. At Admiralty House it was certainly believed that he could and should. Adenaur's own coalition parties had asked him not to go to Paris and, when he did, pursued him with telegrams beseeching him to stand firm and not to sign the treaty without a guarantee that the British negotiations would go on.

But the old man never had the slightest intention of renouncing something which seemed to him infinitely more important than the Brussels transaction. In truth, the Franco–German 'reconciliation' had very little international significance, for there had long since ceased to be any danger of a Franco–German conflict. But there had been a time, and Adenauer still lived with it, when the emnity between France and Germany was the biggest threat to peace. The world had changed faster than the old man's mind. Nothing his European or American colleagues could say or do would have prevailed on him to postpone what he regarded as the consecration of the France–German marriage.

Other statesmen might have found the whole business embarrassing: not Adenauer. On the night of 22 January, after the treaty had been signed and accolades exchanged, he told his entourage that it had been the happiest day of his life.

The Chancellor's party were much less ecstatic. At the ceremonial signing, de Gaulle had kissed Adenauer on both cheeks and only shaken Schroeder's hand saying: 'I do not kiss you, but the sentiments are the same.' If so, they were not reciprocated. Although the German foreign minister, unlike Dr Erhard, was not locked in battle with the Chancellor, he never doubted in his own mind that German links with the United States were far more important than her links with France.

There is no doubt that Adenauer, both in his private talks with the General and afterwards in the presence of his ministers, did insist that he was very worried about the breakdown in Brussels.

The General was sympathetic and attentive. He reminded the old man that he had been insulted by Macmillan, who had come to Rambouillet and talked in detail about world affairs but had kept secret his plans for doing a deal with Kennedy. The Chancellor agreed that this was improper, but said he was not at all surprised. Had not he himself, in February 1959, sent to London his senior foreign adviser the well-known anglophile Dr von Scherpenberg, who had been received by key British officials without being given the slightest hint that, the very day after he got back to Bonn, the Prime Minister was going to announce plans to visit Khrushchev?

The two men agreed that the way things were going it looked as if Labour would soon take over in Britain and that it was hard to say what would happen to the Community if it was enlarged to take in a whole block of neutralists and socialists.

Again the Chancellor went back to the attack: there would be a lot of trouble in Germany if the Brussels negotiations collapsed. Again the General was sympathetic. Then why not delay things a little? What was there to prevent a special group, perhaps the Commission, from being entrusted with a big survey, not only of the state of the negotiations with Britain but of the effect on the community of its enlargement from six to ten? Adenauer thought the idea splendid and came home convinced he had won his point.

Heath returned to Brussels on the evening of the 27th. There he called off a dinner with the former U.S. Secretary of State Christian Herter, now President Kennedy's special envoy for the new tariff negotiations, and instead dined with Erhard. The two men agreed on a scheme for getting the commission to do a rapid report on the state of the negotiations, after which the seven-power ministerial meetings would resume.

Monday, the day the conference was due to reconvene, turned out dark and foggy. The German foreign minister arrived several hours late and had to be diverted to another airport. Coming by car to Brussels he drove immediately to the French mission. There for ninety minutes he and Couve argued on the nature of the de Gaulle–Adenauer agreement. Couve was adamant: the negotiations were finished. The proposed survey was just a decent way of burying them. There could be no question of reconvening the seven. The report would merely be circulated among the Six, who would then take another look at alternative arrangements for maintaining their trade with Britain.

Schroeder saw that this was the end. He telephoned Adenauer. 'Impossible,' said the Chancellor, 'there must be a misunderstanding. You should tell Couve to telephone personally to de Gaulle.'

Schroeder and Couve went together to the conference room where the Six were meeting alone. The procedural wrangle lasted from 7 p.m. till almost midnight: Couve's instructions from Paris obviously left him no room for manoeuvre.

Next morning, the Germans had a last try. Schroeder and Erhard invited Couve to their own embassy. They were engaged in a heated argument when Erhard was called out: it was Mr Tuthill, the U.S. Ambassador, calling with a personal message from Secretary Rusk. The Americans wished the Germans to know that they would consider a rupture as a dangerous blow to the Western alliance. There were no threats in the message, but the implications were clear: the Germans had better be careful. There was no law which forced the Americans to keep almost half a million soldiers with nuclear equipment manning Germany's defences.

In Bonn, German students were picketing the French Embassy. In Moscow, the press was denouncing the military clauses of the Franco–German agreement. In Whitehall and Westminster, Ministers and officials were stunned. And in Brussels after the sad, solemn proceedings we described in the first chapter of this book, Couve was wielding the General's axe.

EPILOGUE

NOBODY was pleased with the ending. The Western alliance and the Kennedy 'Grand Design' were shaken to their foundations. But though this was cheering to the Soviet Union, the Franco–German treaty, with its military and potentially nuclear provisions, gave no cause for comfort to the Russians. The French had forfeited their leading role inside the Community by quarrelling with all their allies. The Germans felt diddled by their old Chancellor, but still too nervous and unsure of themselves to dare get rid of him. The Italians were bitterly resentful of the 'Paris–Bonn' axis. The little countries nursed a sense of grievance and betrayal. A spring had broken in the European Community, and no one knew whether it could ever be repaired. And the British Government was left looking politically naked and ridiculous.

What had gone wrong? Were there any lessons to be drawn from the long sad tale, beyond the confirmation of Puck's dictum: 'Lord what fools these mortals be!'

Britain's mistake, perhaps, was in failing to deal with first things first. Before proposing the revolutionary merger of the British economy into E.E.C., Britain should perhaps have stopped to examine what kind of Europe she wanted and why.

Historically, the decision to apply for entry followed unsuccessful efforts to find other ways of leaping over tariff walls into the lush and growing European markets. The Europeans had insisted on a political commitment and so a political commitment Britain made: at first shamefacedly, then keenly, and finally with booming zeal.

Imperceptibly, the political aspect of the merger ceased to be the means and became the end. The same Prime Minister who had once told Parliament why it would be 'fatal' to British interests for Britain to go in was able to write:

172

Are we now to isolate ourselves from Europe, at a time when our own strength is no longer self-sufficient and when the leading European countries are joining together to build a future of peace and progress instead of wasting themselves in war?

We have to consider the state of the world as it is today, and will be tomorrow, and not in outdated terms of a vanished past. There remain only two national units which can claim to be world powers in their own right, namely the United States and Soviet Russia. To these may soon be added what Napoleon once called 'the sleeping giant' of China, whose combination of rapidly multiplying population and great natural resources must increasingly be reckoned as a potent force in world affairs.

A divided Europe would stand no chance of competing with these great concentrations of power. But in this new European Community, bringing together the manpower, the material resources, and the inventive skills of some of the most advanced countries in the world, a new organization is rapidly developing with the ability to stand on an equal footing with the great power groupings of the world.

No wonder de Gaulle, on that bright June day at Champs in the summer of 1962, thought he and the Prime Minister were talking the same language. Indeed they were. But if the purpose of the new Europe was to create a new superpower to rival the giants, de Gaulle could sensibly ask why it need be permanently intertwined with the Americans? *In*dependence, said the General. No; *inter*dependence, said the Prime Minister. And as the General was inside and the Prime Minister was trying to get in, the General had the last word.

Judged within their own old-world terms of reference, de Gaulle is right. His attitude, inspired, as we have seen in earlier chapters of this book, from a passionate patriotism and from deep belief that a great nation must be in a position to defend itself, may seem silly to younger people, who grew up in the Nuclear Age, when the very concepts of national independence and effective defence are losing reality. Yet it has to be admitted that the General's position, as it emerged from this story, is more consistent and more logical than the Prime Minister's. For if Britain needs its own national nuclear deterrent, as Macmillan asserts, because either the nation's safety or its dignity so requires, why not join with the French and help give them and Britain's other European partners the dignity and safety Britain demands for

173

itself? Are the British non-European as de Gaulle says, and consequently assuming 'Anglo-Saxon' privileges?

As both de Gaulle and Macmillan see it, the case for European union is to make as strong an entity as the United States. These sad old men, leaders of *ci-devant* empires, feel deprived because, in the post-war world, the states they represent no longer rank among the giants. Then why not climb on each other's shoulders and make a collective giant? This was the message of the Prime Minister's pamphlets and of General de Gaulle's press conferences and speeches. Yet the Prime Minister stops short when it is a question of giving the new Europe the nuclear weapons, on which, as the General knows, modern military might depends.

But the real question is not who wins the argument, but whether the argument itself is relevant to the world in which we now live? The British people are not really interested in being annexed into a yet more powerful superstate. What is new and valuable in the 'supranational' experiments, still on trial in Brussels and Luxembourg, is not that they create a new big power, but that they are a revolutionary break-away from the old concept that society must be permanently divided into self-contained and mutually hostile nation-states.

For the British people they raise the basic question of whether the problems of social and economic readjustment to the new technical age might not be handled, to greater human advantage, within more appropriate boundaries than the frontiers of the United Kingdom and Eire. To many elderly politicians, on both sides of the Channel, Europe has grotesquely become an end in itself: a golden fleece to be searched for its own sake.

Yet the only real value of European unity is in the contribution it can make to the well-being of the inhabitants of our distracted continent. If it follows the Gaullist pattern in which a group of Western states form a confederal union, based on a strong military foundation and under authoritarian rule, aiming perhaps at ousting the Russians from Eastern Europe and so expanding from the Atlantic to the Urals, then the Europeans would do far better to preserve a lot of disunited and squabbling little nation-states, mercifully cancelling each other out.

Even the threat of nuclear power from such a bloc could increase world tension and so impede the present and still precarious liberal evolution on the communist side, which remains the only hope of human freedom – in our sense of that word – for the Russians and the satellites, who are Europeans too. A European union retarding this progress would be inimical to the best interests of the peoples of Europe.

But a 'supranational' community imposing common rules on member states is an internationalist experiment of a quite different kind. Looking back over the agony of the first half of the twentieth century, the new Europeans were surely right to proclaim that the nation-state had had its day. Politically, it had incited and provided outlets for untold acts of cruelty and destruction. Economically, it had sponsored beggar-thy-neighbour methods of transacting a country's business in total disregard of the impact outside its own frontiers – with the predictable result that it ended by limiting and obstructing everybody's prosperity.

The idea that there are common purposes to be achieved by joint endeavour could, of course, flourish only inside societies which shared the same degree of political evolution. It is too easily assumed that group hostilities are aberrations from normal human behaviour. In fact, as social psychologists have pointed out, the opposite is true. The normal human condition over the ages has been for the individual, dogged by insecurity and fear, to gang up with others – whether within the family, tribe, or nation – and then to make an absolute distinction between the 'in-group' and the 'out-group': between those to be loved and protected, and those to be hated and killed. Domination was an end in itself, with power and glory for the winning side, generally embodied in the person of the leader, the de Gaulle of the time.

But Western society is developing beyond this point. There is general accord on freedom, tolerance, respect for other people, the settlement of differences between groups by non-violent methods, the admission that people from other countries and other races are also human. With this outlook goes the further admission that the rich industrial nations have a collective responsibility for helping to sustain and develop the rest. Admittedly, such principles are honoured as often in the breach as in the observance. But having come round to admitting that Western society is no longer split by group antagonisms, it seemed sensible to the new Europeans that like-minded countries should break down the barriers separating them from each other.

This did not mean they had discovered a new optimum group of six, ten, or eighteen European countries which should henceforward transact all public affairs of the relevant populations together. On the contrary, there were many matters which could be better left to smaller units, to the town, province, or country. There were still other matters, above all defence, which would have to be handled in a global setting.

The European Community took over a specific number of tasks, hitherto done by national governments, and tried to create wider markets and merge their economies for mutual benefit. The rupture in Brussels does not change the basic fact that there are still many things which could be done better within such a setting than within the narrow limits of national frontiers.

In military production, for instance, none of the separate European States can compete with the American complex. American firms exploit their quasi-monopoly to impose harsh terms, to compel the Europeans both to buy weapons they may not need, and to finance American research and development. Europeans have complained they are thrown back on producing boots and barbed wire.

In the difficult job of staying in business, buying cheap and selling dear, large groups plainly have better bargaining power than small: pooled resources are greater than the sum of separate parts.

But the bargaining power itself is only internationally defensible if the collective group shares similar public purposes for using rather than abusing it, for restraining lobbies and admitting international responsibilities, to which private business and national governments might remain indifferent.

Yet if limited combinations of countries with roughly the same purposes and practices are most suitable, for instance, for economic planning, the same is not true of defence, where security needs to be as collective as possible. It is manifestly in the interests of the European Community that the burden should be shared by all those countries who accept the same definition of aggression and the same exclusively defensive purposes.

The partisans of Europe for Europe's sake have suggested that Britain should buy its way back into the E.E.C. by contributing towards a specifically European nuclear deterrent, as though it were desirable for Western Europe to have a separate self-sufficient military power. But surely this directly contradicts the international purposes which, for Britain, make the Community worth while.

It would be unreasonable to expect the British Conservative Party to adjust easily to a revolutionary concept of international-ism which challenges the whole foundation of Western society. It was more in accordance with traditional dogma for its leaders to present the case for entry into E.E.C. either as a matter of trade or else as an indirect route back into big power politics.

What is more remarkable is the total failure of most of the British Labour Party to grasp the significance of the new inter-national experiment. The cult of the nation-state would seem to run counter to the whole socialist idea, yet when the Brussels negotiations broke down, Harold Wilson, the new party leader, was able to say: 'While we are not slamming the door to proposals to advance European unity – indeed we do not rule out the pos-sibility of further proposals on this – we cannot wait around in Brussels. ... We shall make progress in economic or political cooperation, the less we aim at federal or supranational solutions and the more we work in an inter-governmental framework.'

The hostility of the Labour Party to European entanglements is largely prompted by the fear that the Western European Community is intrinsically Catholic and reactionary and that Britain is safer outside. Gaitskell spoke of the 'two faces' of Europe, and indicated that he did not want to get involved with those countries which, in the recent past, had accepted Hitler and Mussolini.

What he did not admit – though it is surely apparent after two world wars – is that this is Britain's face too. The 'non-intervention' principle – the idea of letting other Europeans stew in their own Nazi or Fascist juice – was nonsense even before the thermo-nuclear age.

Until the British Left ceases to be insular and goes back to its internationalist tradition, there is not likely to be much Britain can do about Europe, beyond making the minimum trading arrangements to limit the damage caused by our rejection from the Common Market.

But once there is a clear view of what the functions of a European Community should be, of the type of planning and development which could more rationally be applied within wider-than-national frontiers, and of the methods by which the public could exercise democratic control, then the British will have something to offer which many Europeans will welcome.

Britain's new initiative might come in another bid to join E.E.C., but this time, instead of preliminary deals about kangaroo meat and sultanas, with a clear political agreement on the collective responsibility of the enlarged community to the outside world. Or, if this route is still blocked, then by offering a new deal, which might be more appealing to the Europeans than the Brussels apparatus paralysed by the Gaullist veto.

The problem, for us and them, is to make a Europe fit for Europeans, including ourselves, to live in. It is time for the old men whose upbringing and experience makes it impossible for them to see beyond national frontiers and parochial patriotisms to step aside and let in the light.

CHRONOLOGY

1946	September	Winston Churchill at Zürich calls for Franco–German reconciliation and the creation of a 'United States of Europe', confederated on the Swiss model
1947	January	General Marshall proposes American aid to Europe
1948	April	O.E.E.C. set up, intended to use Marshall Plan funds to induce Europeans to cooperate
1949	May	Council of Europe formed at Strasbourg
1950	May	Robert Schuman, French Foreign Minister, announces that France and West Germany invite other European democracies to join them in placing their coal and steel under a single authority: Italy and Benelux trio agree, Britain declines
1952	February	Same Six sign treaty forming single European Army
1954	August	French National Assembly rejects European Army treaty
1955	June	Messina Conference. Six plan to integrate their national economies and to develop nuclear energy jointly. Britain refuses invitation to attend
1957	March	Signature of Rome Treaties setting up Common Market and Euratom
1958	November	Breakdown of Maudling negotiations for a free-trade area incorporating all O.E.E.C. countries
1959	November	Signature of European Free Trade Association Convention by Seven: Britain, Norway, Sweden, Denmark, Austria, Switzerland, and Portugal
1960	August	Adenauer invites Macmillan to Bonn: Germans urge Britain to join Common Market
1961	31 July	Macmillan informs House of Commons he has

decided Britain should open negotiations for joining Common Market

10 October — Heath makes opening statement in negotiations

1962 14 January — Six agree on their own common agricultural system, protecting Community farmers against outside competition

29 May — First agreement between Britain and Six: provides gradual elimination of Commonwealth preferences for trade in industrial commodities with Canada, Australia, and New Zealand

2 June — De Gaulle–Macmillan meeting at the Château de Champs goes well

2 August — Britain and Six agree that Commonwealth African and Caribbean territories should be eligible for association with E.E.C.

3 August — Britain and Six agree on broad terms for future trade relations with Asian Commonwealth countries

4–5 August — All-night session fails to settle argument on imports of temperate foodstuffs from old Dominions. Meeting recesses for three months

2–9 September — De Gaulle's triumphal tour in Germany

12–19 September — Commonwealth Prime Ministers' conference

2–4 October — Labour Party Conference at Brighton

10–13 October — Conservative Party Conference at Llandudno

24 October — Brussels negotiations reach deadlock over transitional arrangements for readjusting British agriculture to the Community system

1–3 December — Gaitskell visits Paris and indicates Labour hostility to E.E.C.

15–16 December — De Gaulle–Macmillan meeting at Rambouillet: goes badly

17–19 December — Macmillan meets Kennedy at Nassau: agreement on multilateral and multinational Nato deterrents

1963 14 January — General gives press conference declaring Britain is not ripe for Common Market membership

29 January — Couve de Murville obtains indefinite adjournment of the Brussels negotiations.

EUROPEAN INSTITUTIONS

ORGANIZATION FOR EUROPEAN ECONOMIC COOPERATION. founded in 1948 to deal with Marshall Plan and survived to coordinate European economies. Replaced in 1960 by Organization for Economic Cooperation and Development, in which U.S. and Canada who had been observers became full members.

Permanent secretariat in Paris. No parliament.

Membership: Austria, Belgium, Denmark, France, Germany, Greece, Iceland, Irish Republic, Italy, Luxembourg, Netherlands, Norway, Portugal, Spain, Sweden, Switzerland, Turkey, United Kingdom

THE COUNCIL OF EUROPE. Aims at encouraging political cooperation between European parliamentary democracies. Founded in 1949. Permanent secretariat in Strasbourg. Meeting of ministers and consultative assembly of parliamentarians also at Strasbourg.

Member states have signed about forty conventions, including a Convention of Human Rights, and have set up a court to impose common European rules.

Membership as in O.E.E.C. excluding Portugal and Spain

THE EUROPEAN COMMUNITY. Six member states: France, Germany, Italy, Belgium, Netherlands, Luxembourg. Has three separate institutions: *The Coal and Steel Pool*, founded 1950; *The European Economic Community* (the Common Market), founded 1958; *Euratom*, for joint development of nuclear energy, founded 1958.

All these three have their own European executives, the first in Luxembourg and the second two in Brussels. They share a European Parliament and a common Court of Justice

WEST EUROPEAN UNION. The Six Community members and the United Kingdom joined in 1954, after the collapse of plans for a single European Army to provide an alternative framework for German re-armament. Has ministerial council and parliamentary assembly. Secretariat in London.

*Some other Penguin books
are described on the
following pages*

BERLIN: HOSTAGE FOR THE WEST

John Mander

S209

What is the real purpose of Soviet pressure on Berlin? Why has it been the scene of crisis after crisis every since the Declaration in 1945?

In examining the Gordian knot of these times John Mander, author of *The Eagle and the Bear*, begins by reviewing the events in the former German capital during the past seventeen years. He then lights up, one by one, the three faces of this intractable question. For Berlin is, first and foremost, a pawn in the everlasting chess tournament between Russia and America; secondly, the city constitutes an acute domestic problem for the Germans themselves, whether of the East or the West; thirdly, viewed as a European problem, it is capable of unsettling relations within the Common Market countries.

There is evidence that Russia employs Berlin to throw discord into the Western camp. If Britain, France, and the United States slacken their hold on Berlin, then the German intransigence they sometimes deplore can all too easily be corrupted into a virulent nationalism. The West would be split and Europe would return to the apprehension of the thirties.

TORTURE: CANCER OF DEMOCRACY
FRANCE AND ALGERIA 1954–62

Pierre Vidal-Naquet

S215

In June 1957 Maurice Audin, a brilliant young mathematician, was seized without warrant by French paratroopers, tortured as a matter of routine, and almost certainly murdered a few days later. For in Algeria torture was employed as an instrument of intelligence.

If you feel inclined to say: 'But it can't happen here,' you should read this closely documented book. In it Pierre Vidal-Naquet traces the course of an ugly regression whereby torture, once re-admitted as an instrument of policy, tended to establish itself in a general conspiracy of guilt and silence throughout the French administration, the law, and the Press.

But the shadow does not only lie on France. We, too, set a foot on the same path in Kenya and Cyprus. One must ask whether any democracy can stoop to such barbarities and survive? Or must brutality and the use of torture inescapably lead to policies of hugger-mugger and the ultimate gagging of truth?

PERSECUTION 1961

Peter Benenson

S200

Persecution 1961 contains nine case studies of persecution, intolerance, and brutality in the divided world of the mid-century. Each case shows what can happen to people living under any system of government and law whose views are unacceptable to their rulers or unpopular with their neighbours. The disappearance of Olga Ivinskaya and the imprisonment of Constantin Noica are matched on the other side of the ideological fence by the savage persecution of the Rev. Ashton Jones in America and the appalling humiliation for France of the torture and death of Maurice Audin.

If the worth of human life (dressed in whatever colour of skin) is still to be measured in terms of individual freedom under the rule of a just law, then the price of that freedom is still eternal vigilance, and through Audin's fate, the imprisonment of Patrick Duncan, the flogging of Neto, and indeed all the case studies presented here *Persecution 1961* shows the classic warning to be an urgent and inescapable task of our time.

VOTERS, PARTIES, AND LEADERS
THE SOCIAL FABRIC OF BRITISH POLITICS

Jean Blondel

A638

Are we witnessing the end of class-barriers in the political behaviour of the British voter? Does the businessman vote like the railwayman, the white-collar worker like the unskilled labourer?

Of course they do not. But how different are their voting habits? Trade Unions are Labour inclined, but all trade unionists are not Labour men. Are these non-Labour trade unionists exceptional. And, at the other end of the scale, are Labour-inclined professional people, managers, and executives rare but interesting exceptions?

These are some of the questions which the newly appointed Professor of Government in the University of Essex attempts to answer in this original book. In examining the background, outlook, and interests of voters, party members, politicians, civil servants, and party leaders, and endeavouring to trace some of the subtle threads that tie certain individuals to certain organizations, he presents an anatomy of the political world. And he asks: 'What is the "Establishment" we talk of? Does it exist? And if so, does it rule?'

BRITAIN IN THE SIXTIES: VAGRANCY

Philip O'Connor

S219

Every night, in London, more than 1,000 men sleep rough. Why, amid the upholstery of the welfare state, are there still tramps? Are these men philosophers – devotees of a total liberty? Is their way of life a protest against the strait-jacket of technological society? Are they mentally sick, or does society force them to be pariahs? Are they the tail-end of a long tradition of wandering saints, or plain idle?

Philip O'Connor was 'on the roads' for two years at a stretch and has since returned to the highway on occasions. In this remarkable Penguin Special he gives us the whole world of the vagrant and introduces a colourful flotsam of figures, from the 'model' tramp or the gipsy of seventy-nine to the retired major addicted to 'meths'. He discusses the old Poor Laws and takes us round Rowton House and the reception centres to meet the officials, wardens, and philanthropists who cater for today's down-and-outs.

This compelling study is written with all the intensity and insight of the lonely thinker.

UNARMED VICTORY

Bertrand Russell

S220

We have recently witnessed an unarmed victory of historic significance. The outcome of the Cuban crisis and of the frontier dispute between China and India has proved that the greatest powers, even when they have consolidated a position of strength, may still fight shy of the irremediable lunacy of modern war. The Russians and the Chinese voluntarily accepted compromise without loss of face.

In addressing himself directly to Kennedy, Khrushchev, Nehru, and Chou En-Lai, Bertrand Russell valiantly interposed the small voice of reason during those frightening weeks when we awoke every morning to the prospect of universal annihilation. In substance his proposals – as any reader of this Penguin Special can see – were calculated to achieve exactly what took place. The Russians never challenged the American blockade of Cuba and the guns were rested on the Himalayas.

Would it be too sanguine to conclude that the voice of one of the greatest thinkers of our time was heeded in the chancelleries? At any rate one reads this account of what one man did when the world was swaying on the brink of nuclear war with admiration and gratitude.

THE STAGNANT SOCIETY

Michael Shanks

A555

On its publication as a Penguin Special *The Stagnant Society* received such extraordinary notice from the Press that it was decided to republish as a Pelican this constructive and well-informed comment on the social, economic, and political attitudes of Britain.

'This is the most outspoken, sensible and sympathetic account of what has gone wrong in the unions that I have ever read' – R. H. S Crossman in the *New Statesman*

'His suggested reforms, too, seem eminently sensible – indeed the chief ... characteristics of the whole book are its clarity and common sense' – *Sunday Telegraph*

'It should be compulsory reading for politicians, employers, and trade unionists' – Nora Beloff in the *Observer*

'Mr Shanks has produced a challenging and most timely book. It is excellently written, in clear, crisp, and businesslike prose. ... What Mr Shanks says about more technological and technical training and research and development is all excellent' – Sir Roy Harrod in *The Financial Times*

'It contains much shrewd and effective criticism' – *Guardian* Leader

WORLD EVENTS - 1961
THE ANNUAL REGISTER OF THE YEAR 1960

Edited by Sir Ivison Macadam

R22

This is the 202nd volume of what has become the world's best-known international Year Book. Founded by Edmund Burke as *The Annual Register* in 1758, *World Events* has the longest history of periodical publications in the United Kingdom. Its reliability and authority are undoubted, and learned societies such as the Royal Institute of International Affairs, the Arts Council, the British Association, and the Royal Horticultural Society nominate members of the Editorial Advisory Board.

A precise record of events in a multitude of spheres from politics and law to science and the arts, *World Events* is specially prepared for those who like to be well informed. It is not a mere catalogue of facts, but a collection of concise and readable accounts of all the important happenings of 1960.

Also available:

WORLD EVENTS, 1960

R17